AN ANTHROPOLOGY
OF READING

AN ANTHROPOLOGY OF READING

ERIC LIVINGSTON

INDIANA UNIVERSITY PRESS

Bloomington and Indianapolis

The paper used in this publication meets the minimum requirements of American National Standard for Information Sciences—Permanence of Paper for Printed Library Materials, ANSI Z39.48-1984.

Manufactured in the United States of America.

Library of Congress Cataloging-in-Publication Data

Livingston, Eric.
    An anthropology of reading / Eric Livingston.
       p.   cm.
    Includes index.
    ISBN 0-253-33509-4
    1. English poetry—20th century—History and criticism—Theory, etc.
2. American poetry—History and criticism—Theory. 3. Literature and anthropology. 4. Criticism—Authorship. 5. Poetry—Translating. 6. Books and reading. I. Title.
PR601.L58 1995
801'.95—dc20   94-39577

1 2 3 4 5 00 99 98 97 96 95

Dedicated to Michelle Arens

CONTENTS

PREFACE

Literary criticism takes the activity of reading as the object of its worldly researches: every critical article makes claims about how texts can be read; every reference to prosodic structure, to plot, to rhetorical figures, to meaning, and to reading itself is a reference to how readers read; issues of how reading is done, how it can be done, and how it should be done dominate current critical theory, giving witness to the centrality of reading all along. Yet, to lay readers, the achievements of the discipline are questionable, in one particular way. In literary criticism, reading loses its familiarity as a definite and practical activity. Rather than showing, in detail, how a particular text can be read, critical writings seem to address obliquely the tasks of reading, and to invite the reader into the concerns of a professional discipline. The lay reader must first understand how the literary critic reads in order to understand that reading-really is at issue.

This perception of literary criticism was part of my experience as a student interested in modern poetry and literature. It has taken me a long time to realize its origins and significance. Lay and professional readers, in fact, belong to two different cultures of reading, neither completely distinct, both laying claim to what the practices of ordinary reading are. This book is an attempt to understand these cultures of reading, the relationship between them, and the practices of reading that bind the members of the critical community together.

Rather than relying on general arguments, I have engaged in the careful reading of texts, thereby opening up the practices of reading for inspection. Ethnographic descriptions, cultural artifacts, and descriptive analyses have been brought together so as to exhibit as much as to explain the grounds of an anthropology of reading. Layers of academic discourse about reading had to be removed in order to return the discussion of reading to the phenomena of reading itself. The coherence that I sought, and the project that underlies this book, is the demonstration that professional criticism can, in fact, be examined as a culture of reading practice. I have tried to clarify the worldliness of literary criticism and to show how criticism understands itself as the study of reading-really.

ACKNOWLEDGMENTS

First and foremost, I thank Michelle Arens for her collaboration, her editorial assistance, and her constant support. This book could not have been written without her help.

I am deeply indebted to Harold Garfinkel. Many of the themes in the book come from him—among them, the examination of the "work" of an activity, the natural analyzability of practical action, the relevance of "order terms" and "competent systems," and the investigation of the disciplines as arts and sciences of practical action and reasoning. Much of the terminology is his as well. My graduate studies of poetic and exegetical craft during the 1970s, which provided the origins of this book, were done under his supervision. His work has deeply informed my formulations of a poetic and of a critics' object. Garfinkel's influence, however, is even more pervasive, involving the type of phenomena that are examined, the manner in which they are analyzed, and the vision of ethnomethodology that underlies those analyses.

A considerable portion of this book developed as a dialogue with the writings of Calvin Bedient on the opening of *The Waste Land*. The detailed character of his reading, perhaps unique in the literature, forced me to consider the seriousness and depth of reading found in literary studies. That same detail has allowed me to be critical. I have been critical, but acknowledge here both my indebtedness and my appreciation.

I thank Melvin Pollner for his help in my studies. His lectures on ethnomethodology and phenomenology gave me access to the real-worldly descriptiveness of modern art. His instruction, along with Garfinkel's, also clarified a central problem that this book addresses—the difficulty of exhibiting and analyzing the intrinsic workings of a culture while remaining faithful to its members' practices and to their formulations of those practices.

Martin Krieger's recent work on physics gave me enabling license to put my work together in my own way. His friendship has sustained me; his advice and criticism have always stood me in good stead. Dušan Bjelić's studies of the demonstrations of Galilean science allowed me to realize and shape the material in chapter 3 as an "exegetical demonstration." The treatment of Muybridge's photographic sequences in chapter 8 borrows heavily from his work; his suggestion that ethnomethodologists are alchemists of practice provided one of the central metaphors used in this book. For all this, I am deeply grateful.

In my early studies of poetic craft, I drew inspiration from the poetry and critical writings of Ezra Pound. The influence is still present; I acknowledge here my indebtedness.

Martin Krieger, Charles Livingston, and Rosetta Livingston read and commented on the entire manuscript. Herbert Livingston provided the basic idea of "A Day with Amy" in chapter 8; modifications were introduced to make the story more appropriate to the context. The comments and suggestions of an anonymous reviewer greatly improved the book. Harry Collins, Randall Collins, Graham Cox, and Michael Lynch commented on versions of a paper from which this book, in part, developed. Emanuel Schegloff and Melvin Seeman gave valuable commentary on my earlier work. I thank Peter Hopkins for his assistance and friendship over many years, and Anthony Giddens and Christopher Rojek for reading the manuscript and encouraging me to seek publication.

Trish Battin gave generously of her time to develop the figures for the book, subject to ever-changing specifications and my need to always have them "now." I am indebted to her for her help. Maree Jackes assisted in the few instances when Ms. Battin reached the limits of her software's capabilities.

Mary Jo Johnson has been a special friend over many years; Melvin Seeman's friendship and support have been unwavering since my days as a student. I am deeply indebted in many ways to others as well, among them Joseph Goguen, David Gooding, Mark Gottdiener, Lynn Greenfield, Bruno Latour, Maureen McConaghy, Anita Pomerantz, Carolyn and Richard Rosenstein, Wes Sharrock, Mike Smith, Michael Thompson, Rod Watson, and Steve Woolgar. I have been helped by so many people that I cannot hope to list them all. Steven Thiele, a more recent friend, gave much support when my computer and this book seemed to be coming apart. The debt to my parents and brothers Charles and Lewis goes without saying.

On an institutional level, I am grateful to MIT and Exxon for an Exxon Research Fellowship in the Program in Science, Technology and Society at MIT; to Alumni Services, Inc. for employment during leaner years; to UCLA Extension for my first teaching position; to the Department of Sociology, University of California, Riverside, for an appointment as Visiting Assistant Professor; to the School of Social Science, University of Bath, for a year of teaching and research; and to the University of New England, Armidale, for providing me a home to work and teach.

I am grateful to the following for permission to quote from their books and articles (in alphabetical order of author):

I am indebted to Calvin Bedient and The University of Chicago Press for permission to quote from Calvin Bedient, *He Do the Police in Different Voices: "The Waste Land" and Its Protagonist.* © 1986 by The University of Chicago. Chicago and London: The University of Chicago, 1986.

The quotations from Brooker and Bentley: Reprinted from *Reading "The Waste Land": Modernism and the Limits of Interpretation,* by Jewel Spears Brooker and Joseph Bentley (Amherst: University of Massachusetts Press, 1990), copyright © 1990 by The University of Massachusetts Press.

The quotations from Cleanth Brooks: Reprinted from *Modern Poetry and the Tradition,* by Cleanth Brooks. Chapel Hill: The University of North Carolina Press, 1939.

I thank Oxford University Press for their permission to quote from Robert G. Crowder's *The Psychology of Reading.*

The quotation from Elizabeth Drew: Reprinted with permission of Charles Scribner's Sons, an imprint of Macmillan Publishing Company, from *T. S. Eliot: The Design of His Poetry* by Elizabeth Drew. Copyright 1949 Charles Scribner's Sons; copyright renewed © 1977 William H. Brownell. Eyre & Spottiswood Ltd. offered no objection to the present use of the material.

I am deeply indebted to Harcourt Brace & Company and to Faber & Faber Ltd. for permission to quote from the works of T. S. Eliot and from other authors.

I am indebted to Eugene Wildman for permission to reproduce "death poem #3" by Carl Fernbach-Flarsheim, appearing in Eugene Wildman, ed., *The Chicago Review Anthology of Concretism* (Chicago: The Swallow Press, 1967).

The poem "Fortunatus the R. A." by Dudley Fitts: Dudley Fitts, *Poems from the Greek Anthology.* Copyright 1938, 1941 by New Directions Pub. Corp. Reprinted by permission of New Directions Pub. Corp.

To the University of Michigan Press for permission to quote from Harvey Gross, *Sound and Form in Modern Poetry: A Study of Prosody from Thomas Hardy to Robert Lowell* (Ann Arbor: University of Michigan Press, 1973). Copyright © 1964.

Florence Jones, "T. S. Eliot among the Prophets," *American Literature* 38, 1966. Durham, N.C.: Duke University Press. Reprinted with permission of the publisher.

To Routledge and Kegan Paul for permission to reproduce the illustration from K. Koffka, *Principles of Gestalt Psychology* (London: Routledge & Kegan Paul Ltd., 1935), that appears on p. 7 of this book.

From John T. Mayer, *"The Waste Land:* Eliot's Play of Voices," in *Critical Essays on T. S. Eliot's "The Waste Land,"* edited by Lois A. Cuddy and David H. Hirsch. Copyright © 1991 by G. K. Hall & Co. Used by permission of G. K. Hall & Co., an imprint of Macmillan Publishing Company.

The Wilfred Owen poem "Elegy in April and September (jabbered among the trees)": Wilfred Owen, *The Collected Poems of Wilfred Owen.* Copyright © 1963 by Chatto & Windus Ltd. Reprinted by permission of New Directions Pub. Corp. Random House UK Limited had no objection to the use of the poem.

I am indebted to Grover Smith and The University of Chicago Press for permission to quote Grover Smith, *T. S. Eliot's Poetry and Plays: A Study in Sources and Meaning.* Copyright © 1950 and 1956 by Grover Smith. Chicago and London: The University of Chicago Press, 1956.

The lines from "Sunday Morning": from *Collected Poems* by Wallace Stevens. Copyright 1923 and renewed 1951 by Wallace Stevens. Reprinted by permission of Alfred A. Knopf, Inc. I thank Faber & Faber Ltd. for their permission to quote from this poem as well.

The poem "First there was the lamb on knocking knees" and selected lines from other poems by Dylan Thomas: Dylan Thomas, *Poems of Dylan Thomas.* Copyright 1939 by New Directions Pub. Corp.; 1945 by The Trustees for the Copyrights of Dylan Thomas. Reprinted by permission of New Directions Pub. Corp.

To Thames & Hudson Ltd. for permission to quote William York Tindall, *A Reader's Guide to Dylan Thomas.* Copyright © 1962. London: Thames & Hudson Ltd., 1962.

To Princeton University Press for permission to quote John B. Vickery, *The Literary Impact of "The Golden Bough"* (Princeton: Princeton University Press, 1973).

I thank Dover Publications, Inc. for their assistance and for indicating that the photographic sequences "Man Running" and "Woman Sweeping with Broom" by Eadweard Muybridge are now in the public domain. Both sequences can be found in Eadweard Muybridge, *The Human Figure in Motion* (New York: Dover Publications, Inc., 1955).

I thank Michelle Johnson, Permissions Editor, an unknown archivist, and Prentice-Hall, Inc. for their help in trying to obtain permissions for various photographs that appear in books copyrighted by Prentice-Hall, Inc. My inability to arrange the permissions in no way reflects the efforts they made on my behalf.

In the course of obtaining permissions, I have been the recipient of much kindness and generosity from authors, editors, permission assistants, managers and controllers, and publishers. The list is long. I hope they accept in this way my heartfelt appreciation.

PROLOGUE

When we read a popular novel, an advertisement, or the newspaper, we engage, quite literally, in a certain type of work. The ordinariness of that work allows us to be engrossed in what we are reading; we need not reflectively consider all the things that we are doing. The ordinariness of that work also makes the use of the word "work" seem extreme. Nevertheless, reading does consist of work, and that work can be problematic: we notice that the typesetter has mixed up some of the letters or words, that a verb tense is wrong, that a story makes an inexplicable jump. The discovery of such errors reveals how closely we attend to the work of reading; the people on the morning train show us how absorbing that work can be; any primary school teacher can tell us that the skills of reading must be learned.

Reading animates the critical community, and the arts of reading give familiarity and place, substance and direction to the activities of its members. Yet, the work of reading done by the academic literary critic and that done by the morning commuter are different. When the literary critic discusses a reading of a poem, "reading" refers to a subtle distortion of the laic skills of reading, a kind of alchemy of the practices of ordinary reading. Always performed on a specific text, this alchemy reveals how a particular text can be read. The subtlety arises in that the achievement of this alchemy—that a specific text can be read in a particular way—is, once again, a reference to the skills of ordinary reading. A word such as "art," "science," or "technology" might be used instead of "alchemy"; "cultivation," "culturation," "reconfiguration," or "enrichment" might replace "distortion." But the skills of ordinary and professional reading are so interwoven, and the aims of professional reading are so tied to showing that a text can be re-embedded in reading's ordinary work, that the image of the literary critic as alchemist, reforging the laic skills of reading, seems appropriate.

The word "alchemy" is appropriate in another sense as well. The inseparability of ordinary and professional reading within literary criticism provides the critical enterprise with the object of its endless fascination—the discipline's own practices of reading. Literary criticism is directed to the study of reading-really, but the discipline's own practices of reading are continually projected and seen as reading-really. Terms such as "cabalism," "misreading," "transformation," "intertextuality," and "deconstruction" come to be applied to the arts of ordinary reading and poetic composition where their primary referents are the academic community's own alchemy of reading practice. In studying reading-really, the critical community, in fact, ends up studying itself; in studying its own practices of reading, the discipline sees itself as examining reading-really.

This book is a beginning anthropology of reading; it examines this conundrum of lay and professional practice. In a concrete way, the book shows how the ordinary practices of reading consist of work, how literary criticism is an alchemy of the laic practices of reading, and how criticism takes its own alchemy of reading as its fundamental domain of phenomena and inquiry. It is a book of field work which—by remaining faithful to the cultural practices that it describes, by piecing together descriptions and interrogations of those practices, and through its own alchemy of working with concrete materials—gives a general picture of the culture of academic, critical reading.

AN ANTHROPOLOGY
OF READING

1.

AN ANTHROPOLOGY OF READING

The writings of academic literary criticism have the form of reasoned discourse and rhetorical disputation. Literary criticism is written as an argument, and typically that argument refers to the critical literature as its enabling vehicle. The argument may involve the reading of a particular text:

> Though much has been written on *The Waste Land*, it will not be difficult to show that most of its critics misconceive entirely the theme and the structure of the poem.[1]

The argument may concern a tendentiously agreed upon feature of a text which, although a matter of consensus, needs further examination and elucidation:

> However divergent, all these interpretations agree that what characterizes Lautréamont's verbal behavior is exaggeration: in everything he writes he goes too far, seeking either to parody or to shock.[2]

Or the argument may relate to more general practices of the discipline:

> The first two volumes of the Milton *Variorum Commentary* have now appeared, and I find them endlessly fascinating. My interest, however, is not in the questions they manage to resolve (although these are many) but in the theoretical assumptions which are responsible for their occasional failures.[3]

The reasoned character of professional, critical writing pervades the critical text. It is found not only in general arguments but in the detailed texture of a critical article's thematic development. Each article reveals a surprising density of rhetorical devices.

Consider the discussion of the opening of *The Waste Land* in Cleanth Brooks's "*The Waste Land:* Critique of the Myth." First, there is an ambiguity in stated theme:

The first section of "The Burial of the Dead" [the first part of *The Waste Land*] develops the theme of the attractiveness of death, or of the difficulty in rousing oneself from the death in life in which the people of the waste land live. Men are afraid to live in reality.[4]

Following this, Brooks uses the similarity of metaphor and theme between different works to clarify the meaning of the poem, strengthening his argument with a multiplicity of cited references:

April, the month of rebirth, is not the most joyful season but the cruelest. Winter at least kept us warm in forgetful snow. The idea is one which Eliot has stressed elsewhere. Earlier in "Gerontion" he had written

[. . .
Swaddled with darkness.] In the juvescence of the year
Came Christ the tiger
. . . .
The tiger springs in the new year. Us he devours. . . .

More lately, in *Murder in the Cathedral,* he has the chorus say

We do not wish anything to happen.
Seven years we have lived quietly,
Succeeded in avoiding notice,
Living and partly living.

And in another passage: "Now I fear disturbance of the quiet seasons." Men dislike to be roused from their death-in-life.
The first part of "The Burial of the Dead" introduces this theme through a sort of reverie on the part of the protagonist. . . .[5]

Brooks then leads the protagonist through highlighted passages in the poem. An independent explanation is offered for why the protagonist's reverie is not a coherent whole, and lines 19–24 of the poem, introduced as the resumption of the protagonist's reverie, are reformatted as part of Brooks's argument: lines 19–20 are quoted, but with the end of line 20, "Son of man," removed; a comment—"The protagonist answers for himself"—is interposed; the passage then continues, but with the last word, "Only," deleted. Brooks, in effect, delimits a question and an answer, turning a rhetorical question posed with the force of biblical prophecy into a question that a musing protagonist asks and immediately answers himself, referring to himself as "Son of man." *The Waste Land* reads:[6]

What are the roots that clutch, what branches grow
Out of this stony rubbish? Son of man,
You cannot say, or guess, for you know only
A heap of broken images, where the sun beats,

> And the dead tree gives no shelter, the cricket no relief,
> And the dry stone no sound of water. Only

Reshaped as it appears on Brooks's page, and in that context, the passage becomes an illustration of, and evidence for, a protagonist's reflective daydream.

Brooks's consideration of this passage continues. Eliot refers to Ezekiel 2:1 in his notes to *The Waste Land.* Brooks extends the reference, and juxtaposes the two texts, in the hope, one assumes, that the reader will find how they clarify each other.

> In this passage there are references to Ezekiel and to Ecclesiastes, and these references indicate what it is that men no longer know: The passage referred to in Ezekiel 2, pictures a world thoroughly secularized:
> 1. And he said unto me, Son of man, stand upon thy feet, and I will speak unto thee.
> 2. And the spirit entered into me when he spake unto me, and set me upon my feet, that I heard him that spake unto me.
> 3. And he said unto me, Son of man, I send thee to the children of Israel, to a rebellious nation that hath rebelled against me: they and their fathers have transgressed against me, even unto this very day.[7]

A mischaracterization of the lines from Ezekiel is also involved: a completely secularized world is not the same as a world in which the children of Israel have rebelled and transgressed against their god. Moreover, while the "protagonist" does describe a "secularized world"—one without deeper significance or symbolic meaning—this characterization misses the detailed picture that the "protagonist" gives of that world. In that strange reversal of analysis for motivation, Brooks's characterizations of the protagonist's speech are offered as the essential meaning that the protagonist seeks to convey. In addition, Brooks further adumbrates Eliot's text, selectively quoting it for the purposes of his argument. The dramatic message that is delivered at the end of this part of the text has been avoided, and therein the need to explain it. Oddly, this message gives force to Brooks's claim that this section of the stanza concerns a secularized world and the secularized life of its inhabitants.

In the science demonstration in which one child is the nucleus of an atom and another, on the far side of the playground, is an electron, absence dominates rather than presence. Looked at closely, the substance of Brooks's argument seems ephemeral rather than solid; only the constructed coherence and continuity of the argument remain. Brooks's reasoned discourse appears to reflect, using a current idiom, an underlying will to knowledge, embedded in scholarly discipline and expressed in the language of insight and truth.

A different type of analysis is provided by Calvin Bedient's commentary on the opening seven lines of *The Waste Land:*

> Paradox and *non sequitur* between them divide up the opening block, the first saying that "happiness" (the low dream) is misery; the second, that a secular existence does not add up. Under the aegis of the first, the lively *incipit* of Chaucer's *Canterbury Tales* (virtually the *incipit* of English poetry) is turned on its head in "April is the cruellest month." To rhyme "April" with "cruel"! April breeds lilacs out of the "dead land"? Isn't that a black magic? "Winter kept us warm"? Here logic grimaces. There is logical chagrin, too, in the fancy of feeding a little life with dried tubers. This approaches conundrum, a mad science. In all, a topsy-turviness. Even English prosody is queered as the first three lines fall a syllable short of iambic pentameter, in a resistant way, and the fourth—with its stubborn pull and push of monosyllables, "Dull roots with spring rain"—seems intractably to stop at the halfway point of a decasyllabic. The accentual tug and clot of "Dull roots" tries to hold its own against the resonant drumming of "spring rain," with only the filmy, flimsy "with" to stand in between. Deceptive Chaucerian beauty of measure is flouted, no line is an "expected" English line, love itself is not what the "dark shimmer of sex" portends.[8]

Bedient's analysis illustrates the complexity of critical argumentation. Bedient wishes to characterize the opening lines of *The Waste Land* as consisting of paradoxes; to do so, he evokes a conventional comparison of the lines with those of the Prologue of *The Canterbury Tales*. In part, Bedient substantiates the relationship between the two texts through a scansion of Eliot's lines—"the first three lines fall a syllable short of iambic pentameter"—with the implication that Chaucer's lines might be read as strict iambic pentameter. As Bedient indicates, however, the relationship between the texts is anything but straightforward, lying as much in their differences as in their similarities. Bedient's central rhetorical device is that these differences were purposely intended by Eliot. The device is not made explicit but concealed within Bedient's description of the text—"the lively *incipit* of Chaucer's *Canterbury Tales* . . . is turned on its head in 'April is the cruellest month'"; "Deceptive Chaucerian beauty of measure is flouted."

These features of Bedient's analysis are all tied together, all contributing to a larger purpose. Bedient wishes to distinguish distinct, separate voices in the first stanza of *The Waste Land:* if later lines can be characterized as *non sequiturs*, the opening lines consist of paradoxes; if later lines describe a literal, concrete world, earlier ones reflect an emotional response to life. The first voice speaks in paradoxes and conveys disillusionment and resignation; the utterances of the second voice are *non sequiturs* and describe the surface details of the material world.[9]

Brooks's and Bedient's texts are both examples of reasoned discourse. Both analyses can be read for their cogency and worldliness without consulting *The Waste Land*; that Brooks and Bedient are talking about *The Waste Land* is an achievement of their critical texts. Yet, there is a problem here, for Brooks's and Bedient's analyses are, in fact, very different.

While Brooks's analysis is clear and straightforward, it may be impossible to rescue. The relationship between what Brooks says and an actual reading of *The Waste Land* is vague in almost all its details; the reader must create the meaning of what Brooks says in order to find that he is discussing an actual reading of *The Waste Land* at all. Brooks is presenting a reasoned argument; despite the reasonableness of the story that he tells, it is a narrative about reading, maybe nothing more. Bedient's analysis, on the other hand, seems baroque, in-house, and contrived, if not simply "wrong." The descriptive use of the word "paradox" is, minimally, debatable; the scansion is poor. Although the "low dream of sex"[10] may be misery (if the stanza reflects even this), nowhere does Eliot's text say "'happiness'. . . is misery." In fact, the quotation marks around "happiness" indicate that Bedient recognizes that he is forcing his argument. Yet this equivocation is also an indication that Bedient has before him an actual reading that he is attempting to describe. As we shall see, a concrete way of reading the opening stanza of *The Waste Land* emerges from Bedient's analysis, turning that analysis into sensible commentary on that reading. Therein lies the problem.

Although critical writings have the form of reasoned argumentation, the seriousness of criticism is found in the discovered readings of texts that lie beneath and are evidenced through argumentation. The meritoriousness and value of Brooks's and Bedient's analyses are located in what they teach about reading *The Waste Land*. Literary criticism is about reading. It is about reading as it applies to specific texts, and it is about the reading of those texts. The practices of reading, not argumentation, bind the critical community together and constitute the worldliness of its projects. When the focus is on critical argumentation, the heart of the discipline is lost.

An anthropology of reading begins by clearing away talk about reading to examine the practices of reading themselves; it seeks the phenomena of reading beneath reasoned discourse, and it seeks the origins of reasoned argumentation in the practices of reading. The feasibility of the anthropological project lies in restoring to reading its concreteness as a real activity—the inspectable, cultural practices of a community.

2.

READING'S WORK

In introductory classes in sociology, I often give students the following assignment: as they are walking on a sidewalk with a friend, while continuing to look, talk, and act in a normal manner, they are to angle their trajectories very slightly toward the curb instead of straight ahead. I claim that the friend, in a short time, will be pushed off the sidewalk. The friend may look puzzled, curious, or irritated, or may say something like, "What are you doing?" "You," however, have not done anything, at least not by "yourself." People walking together continually monitor the distance between them as part of what walking together, as an activity, is. The students have simply used this complicity to "manipulate" their friends.

The good fun that can be had with such experiments—turning people in circles while having a conversation, getting them to look over their shoulders, or backing them down a corridor—is not the point. Slightly changing ordinary activities and making them problematic serve to exhibit what people do when the activities are not problematic. Adjusting interpersonal distance, sound level, and general eye contact are practical actions. These actions, and the practical reasoning which accompanies them, make ordinary activities nonproblematic. As we walk, we monitor our relative positions; as we are having a conversation, we continually assess and regulate our interpersonal distance. We actively engage in the "work" of social distance; it contributes to, and is part of, the normality of a normal conversation. "Troublemaking" experiments, such as angling the trajectory while walking, serve only to make this "work" more visible.[1]

I

The following sentence might be considered an experiment similar to the one above. In this case, it illuminates the "work" of reading.

While she was sewing the sleeve fell off her lap.[2]

When we read this sentence, we read it as

While she was sewing the sleeve
  fell off her lap.

We realize that something is wrong with the sentence, and that what is "wrong" involves the word "fell." We look at the sentence and try

the sleeve fell

as a possible kernel for organizing our reading. Then, we check to see if the sentence now makes sense:

While she was sewing
  the sleeve fell off her lap.

Prior to finding this problem of reading, what are readers doing that leads inevitably to the problem? What is it that readers search for in the sentence after they see that it has gone awry?

Psychologists of reading refer to this type of sentence as a "garden-path" sentence: as it is read, the reader anticipates or recognizes a structure for the sentence; the end of the sentence does not support that structure; the reader has been led up a garden path. According to the psychological account, the reader's eyes fixate on the word "fell" for longer than usual; during this time, the reader is processing the information in the text.[3]

Viewed from the perspective of Gestalt psychology, the garden-path sentence might also be said to have "poor continuation." Gestalt psychologists conduct experiments in which parts of a line drawing, for example, are successively removed. The face of a plump, spectacled man is seen in Figure 1.[4] If more details were removed from the illustration, the features of the face

Figure 1

might not be seen as clearly, or be recognized as features of a face at all. What amount of detail is needed for the viewer to be able to fill in what is missing and, thus, for the drawing to have "good continuation"?

The "garden-path" analogy, reinterpreted slightly, suggests that the reader is not simply "led" by the sentence, but actively participates in finding that path. While reading the sentence, the reader is actually developing a method for reading that particular sentence. It is this ongoing constructive process that is being led astray. The Gestalt analogy, on the other hand, suggests that the reader is using the material detail of the text as the grounds for building that method of reading. Some texts supply enough detail to allow them to be read without difficulty; in the sentence about sewing, the material text does not offer sufficient grounds for "good continuation."

Providing a larger context for the original sentence is one way of examining these issues.

> Amy was in a hurry. She placed the sleeve in her lap and started sewing the eyelet. While she was sewing the sleeve fell off her lap.

The problematic character of the sentence has been reduced. The sleeve, by being placed in Amy's lap, is disassociated from the thing that she is sewing, the eyelet. By the time the reader gets to "While she was sewing the sleeve," grounds have been established for seeing the sleeve as something different from what Amy is sewing. The reader has developed a method of reading (and the surrounding text has allowed that development) from within which the problematic sentence is less problematic.

When readers read, they are actively engaged in an activity which might be said to consist of "work." They are doing things while reading, and what they are doing is "work." For the most part, this work is so familiar and ordinary that it does not cause readers to reflect on what they are doing: they read the morning paper as they drink their coffee. It is engaging work, it draws the reader to it, and it requires that attention be paid to it in order for it to get done, but it is not a radically perplexing or debilitating activity.

When the sentence about sewing is isolated from a surrounding context, the sentence is disengaged from the developing pattern of ordinary things that readers do when they read.

> While she was sewing the sleeve fell off her lap.

The reader must begin the work of reading with just this sentence. Moreover, the sentence is constructed so that it interferes with that "work" and with the ordinary course of reading. The sentence is purposely contrived as a "breaching experiment" to disrupt (and therein tacitly acknowledge) how we ordinarily read.

There is, of course, an obvious way of rendering Amy's sewing harmless:

> While she was sewing, the sleeve fell off her lap.

The little mark, the comma, does it all. But what does it do? We could say that it separates the subordinate from the principal clause, but how does it do this?

The comma shows us how to read the sentence by supplying a material trace—a description—of how we should organize our work of reading. As we read "While she was sewing" and then come to the comma, we see the comma as separating the sewing from what follows. The developing organization of our work of reading this particular sentence, with its comma, finds in the material substance of the text—the comma—the grounds for its continuing and developmental organization.

What are we searching for, then, in the original "garden-path" sentence when we come to the word "fell"?

> While she was sewing the sleeve fell off her lap.

We are searching, in the sentence, for the material grounds for organizing our work of reading this sentence. When we find those material grounds— that "the sleeve" can be separated from the "sewing" as the thing that "fell"— we see that the sentence can be read as

> While she was sewing, the sleeve fell off her lap.

We have found the coherence and "good continuation" of *our work* of reading that sentence. We then say that we have understood the sentence and that it now makes sense. At the same time, the sentence without the comma is still seen to be "inherently" troublesome; it is not written so as to provide adequate grounds for organizing the work of reading.

II

In the literatures on teaching children to read and on diagnosing reading problems, the context surrounding a word is recognized as providing clues to its meaning. Farr and Roser, for example, in *Teaching a Child to Read,* offer some illustrations.[5]

In the first example below, context provides a definition of the word "grocery." In the second, "athlete" is given meaning through the adjectives and the noun associated with it. In the third, a comparison (indicated by the word "but") may help identify an aurally familiar word, "evening."

> Mr. Parker owned a grocery, where people came to buy fruit, vegetables, meats, and other foods. He sold soap, pet food, and lots of other things, too.
>
> The strong athlete won the gold medal.
>
> In the bright morning light, Sue could always see who was coming over the hill. But in the gray evening, it was not so easy to tell.

When directed, as we are by Farr and Roser, to attend to the meaning of a specific word, "context" refers to a background which gives clues to the word's meaning. When attention is shifted to the contextual clues themselves, the meaning of individual words is seen as only part of a larger and more complex phenomenon. The sentences about Mr. Parker tell something about owning and selling, about using lists to exhibit an abstraction (food), and about using lists to indicate a generality (all the things in a grocery). In the sentence about the athlete, all the words fit together as stars in a constellation: there is one athlete who, by virtue of being strong, won a medal which was the one gold medal. The last example is more complicated. The fact that a comparison is being made is found in the parallel construction and in the contrasting (and mutually articulating) adjectives "bright" and "gray," as well as in the use of "but." "Seeing" is related not only to "light" but to the ability to "tell" something—to the arts of recognition and description. There is an implied construction in the second sentence—in the gray evening, it was not so easy to tell *who was coming over the hill*—that depends on the parallelism that the sentence, simultaneously, exhibits, and there is a tricky relationship between Sue's being able to see in the morning and the impersonal fact that it is not so easy to see in the evening.

When attention is shifted from the foreground to the background—from the meaning of individual words to the contextual clues themselves—the clues are seen to relate not just to the meaning of separate words but to how all the words work together.

III

Consider the three texts below—"The Painted House,"[6] "The Sentence-Method,"[7] and "Elegy in April and September"[8]—imagining them as pictures laid side by side. What, in terms of the activity of reading, are their essential differences?

The Painted House

The funny little smile on Father's face was something to see. He was having the best time ever, painting his house.

"Yes, that's what I'll paint next," he said to himself. "I'll paint a band of blue for the sky. Then I'll make big splashes of white for the clouds. Then maybe I'll paint silly pictures all over the house."

Before long Mother came into the yard. How she laughed when she saw what Father was doing.

"This will be an odd-looking house," Mother said. "But what a grand idea!"

Mother got some bright yellow paint. She scrunched down on the ground and began to paint flowers on the house.

THE SENTENCE-METHOD. Experiments in Binghamton, New York, in the 1870s were interpreted to support what we might call a "whole-sentence" method of reading instruction. This might seem a *reductio ad absurdum* of the word method, but it was apparently taken seriously by some. Basically, one would expose a sentence to the child visually, at the same time reading it aloud distinctly. Then another sentence both visually and aloud, and so on. As the child noticed the relation between the print and the speech was not random, he or she would gradually be expected to see the correct correspondences, and then to generalize them to fresh samples.

One could defend the sentence method on the grounds that a sentence is a complete idea and, therefore, beginning with any lesser unit forces the child to make unnatural segmentations. Of course, extensions of this logic are staggering—it is really the *paragraph*, it might be claimed, that contains whole ideas, not the individual sentence, therefore. . . .

Elegy in April and September
(jabbered among the trees)

Hush, thrush!
Hush, missen-thrush, I listen . . .
I heard the flush of footsteps through the loose leaves,
And a low whistle by the water's brim.

Be still, daffodil!
And wave me not so bravely.
Your gay gold lily daunts me and deceives,
Who follow gleams more golden and more slim.

Look, brook!
O run and look, O run!
The vain reeds shook . . . Yet search till gray sea heaves,
And I will wind among these fields for him.

Gaze, daisy!
Stare up through haze and glare,
And mark the hazardous stars all dawns and eves,
For my eye withers, and his star wanes dim.

What, in terms of the activity of reading, are the essential differences between these texts? The texts are so different that the question may seem too general or the answer too obvious. The fact that one is a children's story, one is from a textbook, and one is a poem is an inadequate answer: all three have a narrative structure. Moreover, descriptions such as a "children's story" or a "poem" refer to conclusions drawn from the activity of reading, rather than to an essential difference in the activity itself. Why is "The Painted House" so clearly a story for children and "The Sentence-Method" an example from a college textbook? The answer lies in the interrelatedness of the contextual clues. These clues provide a "gestalt texture" for reading's work.

In the children's story, the contextual clues are marked by repetition and redundancy. Not only does Father have a smile on his face, but it is a smile that could be seen. Not only does he think something, he affirms to himself that he thinks it. When Mother laughs, what she is laughing at is explained; while Mother is the only one in the story who could say what she says, the text clarifies that Mother said it. The adjectives are, for the most part, unnecessary and redundant, and the temporality of events, independently of the repeated verbs, bangs like a drum: "next," "then," "then," "before long," "when."

Children need this overdetermination of "contextual clues" because they are learning how to use them. In that children are developing the societal skills of reading pace, eye fixation, and recognition, such clues need to be repeated for them to be clear. The "clues," in effect, provide a description of how the text is to be read. For the competent reader, the description of reading that "The Painted House" provides overdetermines the way that it should be read. Seeing this is part of what it means to be a competent reader.

In contrast to "The Painted House," the sophistication of the "sentence-method" text is apparent from its promissory character and the ways in which its promises are developed and fulfilled. In the opening sentence, various types of doubt are introduced—experiments in Binghamton, New York, "were interpreted" "to support" "what we might call. . . ." The second sentence elaborates this context of doubt, in part by saying that the whole-sentence method is a *reductio ad absurdum* of the "word method." The epito-mizing description of the sentence method (beginning in the third sentence and indicated by the use of "basically") gives an idea of the word method as well; a sense of a *reductio ad absurdum* is given in the last paragraph, which contextually (if not substantively) satisfies the early indications that the whole-sentence method need not be taken seriously.

The "sentence-method" text is an example of a text that is both sophisti-cated and accessible. It actually has as great a density of contextual clues as the children's story. The meaning, for example, of a child's being forced "to make unnatural segmentations" is developed and given sense in the sentence in which the phrase occurs. The difference between the texts is that in the more sophisticated one, the contextual clues are more finely articulated. The contextual clues are not redundant; they do not repeatedly elaborate the same basic description of how the text should be read. If the "gestalt texture" of "The Painted House" overdetermines the way that we should read its story, that of "The Sentence-Method" could be said to be adequate to its reading.

In the case of the third text—like a line drawing in which too many details have been removed—many readers cannot read the poem for its self-elaborat-ing sense. They are reduced to identifying its possible features: Does the poem describe spring? Why is the brook asked to run and look? Where is the speaker of the poem? In contrast to the previous examples, the work of reading "Elegy in April and September" lacks coherence; readers do not find continuity in the way in which they read the text. There are plenty of contextual clues—the speaker appears to be talking to nature, to be listening for things; another person seems to be involved. The clues, however, seem unrelated and do not "go" anywhere. The poem's contextual clues underdetermine the way that it should be read.

The activity of reading is obviously affected by the particular text that is being read, as it is with the three texts above. When we look at the contextual clues, however, the relationship between the text and the activity of reading no longer seems simple. Certainly, this relationship does not consist of a direct correspondence between individual words and their meanings. It in-volves the interrelatedness of the contextual clues themselves.

In the line drawing of the face in Figure 1, the lines provide a "gestalt contexture"—the glasses are glasses because they rest on the nose; the eye-lash is an eyelash because it is behind the glasses and below the eyebrow. The lines are organized so as to fit together to provide a coherent ensemble of the features of a face, and it is through the seen face that these features fit together.[9] The seen and complete face—the gestalt—is neither in nor not in the fragmentary lines; it is in the lines as the perceptual gestalt that the lines themselves are seen to configure. The lines provide the material grounds for the face that is seen.

The interrelatedness of contextual clues in a text provides a similar gestalt "texture" for reading. The interrelatedness of these clues does not lie in the text, but in the activity of reading that uncovers them. Neither, however, does that interrelatedness not lie in the text, but in a text already and always embedded in the activity of reading. The clues fit together to provide a description of how the work of reading should be organized, and the clues are uncovered and fit together, in real time, by the reader, as a developing organization of reading's prosaic work.

We are led to the following reflexive proposition:

> The work of reading is the work of finding the organization of that work that a text describes.

The contextual clues in a text offer the grounds, from within the active, participatory work of reading, for finding how those clues provide an adequate account of how the text should be read.

IV

Texts are usually thought of as physical things, their properties assured independently of the act of reading. Reading, on the other hand, is construed as an operation performed on such objects, the "processing of information" found in a text. Yet, whatever a text's ultimate properties, it takes on its observed properties from within the work of reading. Reading consists of work that is always done in conjunction with a particular text. Rather than having two separate things—texts and reading—the two together constitute one object—a "text/reading" pair.[10]

Reading is always found as a text/reading pair. Every reference to a text in literary criticism, whether to verb tense or to prosodic structure, is a reference to a reading of that text. Conceptually, the pair can be thought of as consisting of two parts: a text and the work of reading. A text, however, is always and already embedded in that work, and from within that work, the text provides "clues" as to how it should be read. Similarly, the work of reading is hopelessly entwined with its text, and reading's work is the work of finding how a text describes its reading. In this way, a text provides an "account" of its own reading; the text is a "reading account," a story about how its own reading should be done.

This pairing of text and reading is done while a reader is reading, and done simply as reading's ordinary, prosaic, unremarkable work. The pairing is made possible by the skills of which ordinary reading consists, revealed in and as the work of reading. A text provides the material grounds through which those skills are organized; a text/reading pair develops as a dynamically emerging "figure" from the background of those skills.[11] A text/reading pair does not reveal prior knowledge but the background of prior, practical skills of reading that a text is found both to require and to organize.

Whether it involves the newspaper or a poem by Wilfred Owen, reading, as an activity, is always the ongoing unfolding of a text/reading pair. In part, the work of reading is recognized in its accomplishments—simply as that which a text can be seen to "say"—in and as that text's transparency, its cleverness, it ambiguousness, or its grammatical nonsense. In part, reading's work is recognized in its practicality: the text "says" what it does insofar as reading finds, in the text, the practical grounds for continuing the further articulation and organization of its work as that particular, developing text/reading pair.

V

Consider the following epigram:

> The loss of money is bewept with genuine tears.[12]

When we read this line, we ask, "Is that it?" What is to be made of the line? The work of reading has become problematic. At the same time, this perception is already embedded in a reading of the text. The single line of text is all that there is, and its obscurity occasions the search for its proper reading. Some time, however short, passes before we see how to read the epigram. Then, as with the problem of the animal-in-the-foliage, we see the satiric smile.

The epigram offers a puzzle, for it depends on what it does not say. When readers pause over the word "genuine," they see that it emphasizes something and ask, "What?" A comparison is being made with those things for which false tears are shed, but the comparison itself is not stated. Through the missing object of an implied comparison, the comparison comes to encompass every other possible occasion of tears.

The puzzle, however, is that this missing contrast only begins to show what is "missing" from the line: that there is a comparison; that the modifier "genuine" signals that comparison; that the line refers to everybody; and that the lost money that everyone beweeps is his or her own money, not someone else's. A huge domain of reading practice looms in the background to which the sense of the epigram is integrally tied.

Being able to read the line for what it says is an achievement, but where does this achievement lie? Certainly not in a mute and distant text, a text that first exhibited its problematic or unfinished character. Not, at least phenomenologically, in the mind of the reader, either: it is not the reader's achievement but, experientially, that of the text for anyone to read. The reader actively searches for an organization of reading's work; the discovery is finding such an organization evinced in the intimate details of the text. The text comes to exhibit its own description of reading's work.

Like the skills of walking together, the skills of reading need specific if, generally, unremarkable attention and monitoring. When children are taught to read, skills are cultivated that bring them into the community of readers. Through any number of devices—group reading, testing, writing—children are taught to actively and attentively implement these communal skills in their own actions, therein becoming the purveyors and sentinels of the society's ways of reading. Reading leaps beyond its textual basis to the thing that is transparently read, and in that leap, in the anonymity of the organized course of reading that is now available, the social character of the phenomenon lies. Children are taught the skills of which that leap consists.

That readers can read the epigram and find its irony speaks of a shared background, not of knowledge but of practical skill: seeing that something is missing, realizing the importance of its being missing, finding what this absence means. That readers are not engaged in an idiosyncratic activity reflects this shared background of skill. Readers do not find their own cleverness but the clever irony of the line. The epigram is read for what it says; it is there for "anyone" who can read. Reading is neither in a text nor in the reader. It consists of social phenomena, known through its achievements which lie between the text and the reader's eye, in the reader's implementation of society's ways of reading, in reading what a text says.

3.

THE EXEGETICAL
DEMONSTRATION

Some texts, such as *The Waste Land*, present serious difficulties for both professional and lay readers. Other texts, including the newspaper, popular fiction, and most of Shakespeare, appear straightforward and unproblematic, but can be shown to hide deep and enigmatic obscurities. These twin phenomena—the open difficulties and the cloaked problems of reading—provide the ever-present motives for professional criticism, often stated in terms of an increased appreciation of "literature" and "culture" or in terms of the aims, the substantive contributions, and the complexities of the critical enterprise. Yet, in their omnipresence throughout literary criticism, these same phenomena would also seem to threaten the foundations of that enterprise. Everywhere the critical eye focuses, reading is open to question. Wherein do the actual achievements of literary criticism lie?

An equally primordial experience sustains the discipline in the face of these phenomena. Consider the following poem by Wilfred Owen, introduced in the preceding chapter.[1]

Elegy in April and September
(jabbered among the trees)

Hush, thrush!
Hush, missen-thrush, I listen . . .
I heard the flush of footsteps through the loose leaves,
And a low whistle by the water's brim.

Be still, daffodil!
And wave me not so bravely.
Your gay gold lily daunts me and deceives,
Who follow gleams more golden and more slim.

Look, brook!
O run and look, O run!
The vain reeds shook . . . Yet search till gray sea heaves,
And I will wind among these fields for him.

Gaze, daisy!
Stare up through haze and glare,
And mark the hazardous stars all dawns and eves,
For my eye withers, and his star wanes dim.

The story behind the poem is that of a sniper who lies in wait to kill an enemy soldier. He asks the birds to be still so that he can listen for footsteps; he asks the flowers not to give away his presence. Eventually, he will find the enemy and kill him.

At first the poem appears as a collection of fragmented lines with little continuity; then, with the aid of a few interpretive remarks, it becomes self-exhibiting of its meaning. The imprecisions of the text become more important than the false precision of the exegesis, and the grounds of the interpretation come to lie not in argumentation but in "seeing" how the text can be read.

This phenomenon of reading is mysterious. The reading of some particular text appears, at first, opaque and fragmented, or clouded by the commentary that has surrounded its reading. A possible inner coherence of a way of reading the text is seen, and the text begins to unfold to its reading, becoming the embodiment of clarity. Experientially, the reading that unfolds is the way in which the text should be read. Rather than the achievement of analysis, the reading appears as an anonymous discovery about reading, available to any competent reader. Therein, that reading also seems eminently teachable: when attention is directed to a few of the text's details, a proper reading becomes obvious. The unanticipated, unprecedented, unplanned character of this reading makes it seem a miracle; its eminent teachability provides the basis of the exegetical demonstration.[2]

Producing such demonstrations and seeing such demonstrations performed sustain the members of the discipline in their work. Each critical article offers itself as containing such a demonstration—whether it is about a specific text, the use of imagery in a particular period, or a feature of the critical literature. The grounds of the literary demonstration lie within the laic skills of ordinary reading. The achievements of such demonstrations, in their most elemental form, are achievements of these laic skills as well. The literary demonstration reveals a "poetic object," a sculpted object of the prosaic arts of reading's work.

I

Ordinary reading has an unfinished, continually unfolding temporality. The phrase "suspension of disbelief" is used to refer to the idea that a reader temporarily dismisses the fictional nonreality of what a text says. The expression has meaning because readers are busy at their work, waiting to find out what comes next and who did what. The attractiveness and prospective fulfillment of this work keep the reader reading.[3]

A "poetic object" has a special property: it has coherence as a completed "thing." In "Elegy in April and September," the temporal unfolding of the story is essential: the reader is, with the speaker of the lines, listening, hiding, searching for what is then revealed as a person that the speaker seeks to kill. This temporal development unfolds, however, only from the perspective of the poem as a unified object. A reader must first find an organization for the work of reading the poem that then allows the poem to be read for its temporal development. The temporality of a poem's depicted action is an achievement of the poetic object.

The wholeness of the poetic object is essential to it. While reading is the work of finding the organization of that work that a text describes, the poetic object adds a self-sustaining completeness to this work. To indicate its character as an object, it is bracketed and written as a [text/reading] pair.[4] As its witnessed achievement, the text of a poetic object provides a precise description of the organization of reading's work that the object itself requires. The manner in which this is done is oblique, through its contextual clues.

In "Elegy in April and September," the text begins by indicating that "Hush, thrush" is not metaphoric; it is said (or thought) for a reason: the speaker of the lines is listening, and listening with a purpose—he has "heard the flush of footsteps." The reader sees that it is an "I" who is saying or thinking this; the ellipsis indicates that he is listening for something. The change of tense from "I listen" to "I heard" indicates that this listening is related to having heard the signs—the footsteps—of another person. The daffodil should be still because it signals the speaker's presence; the brook must "run and look" because the speaker is searching for "him." The other person and the mysteriousness of the speaker's intentions are conveyed through the other's presence only in signs, in possible signs, and in the search for him through those signs.

As the poem develops, the resonances of "bravely," "daunts," and "deceives" lead to the envisioned meeting. In the last line, this meeting bodes ill for both the speaker and the mysterious other, and this gives "hazardous stars" its character as pathetic fallacy: the projected encounter is hazardous, not the stars. At the same time, the position of the speaker and the person he seeks—identified as a man only in the twelfth line—is not a symmetric relationship: one is purposefully hiding, listening, and searching while the other is apparently unaware that he is being sought. This asymmetry provides the grounds for the ending contrast: if things go badly for the speaker, they go worse for the other person.

Underlying these clues, and an integral part of them, is the fact that the poem has a narrative structure: the poem builds through each of the stanzas to the anticipated meeting, but without saying what the nature of that meeting is. The title—what we pass beyond without giving specific attention— tells us that this is an elegy, a lamentation for the dead. April and September may be the time of killing, or they may contrast spring and fall, the natural setting with the anticipated action.

The text of a poetic object describes the work of its reading in this indirect manner, by fitting together its "contextual clues." The organization of reading's work that it offers is a gestalt of reading practice, and the contextual details of the text provide the basis of, and evidence for, that organization. This organization of reading is something "real." It is "massive"; it has "weight." The text can be consulted repeatedly and repeatedly read to find that reading once again and to inspect its finer details. The reading is not the analysis through which it is inexactly described, nor is it the paraphrase which trivializes the reading—"the actions of a dutiful but regretting soldier hunting the enemy."

The poetic object is discovered as a definite method of reading, exhibited through its text. From within the perception of this object, the reader appreciates the artistry of its construction. In Owen's poem, the reader must wait for the last lines to make clear the gestalt of reading that the poem offers. Through this postponement, the "despair" and "fatality" of the last lines take on their forcefulness. The achievement is similar to a "gestalt switch" where the text provides the grounds first for one indefinite way of reading, then for a different, precise one.[5] A reader actively searches for an organization of reading's work; the discovery is finding such an organization evinced in the intimate details of the text. The text comes to exhibit its self-sustaining precision as a description of reading's work. The poetic object is this [text/reading] pair's particular, distinctive accomplishment; it is this poem particularly.

The text of the poetic object is a literal text. It may be a metaphorical text; it may be a self-reflective text; the text's meaning may not be transparent. It is a literal text in that the text describes precisely how it should be read, whether metaphorically, as commentary on itself, or as a construction that suggests a depth of meaning that is not made simple.

Consider the following "poetic object":

> Fortunatus the portrait-painter got twenty sons
> But never one likeness.[6]

Here, the work of reading is the work of "putting together" the strange logic of the text: that Fortunatus is a portrait-painter, that none of his "twenty" sons resemble him, and that he "got" his sons—the odd, incongruous word "got" that reading finds, that overdetermines the picture, and then shows us how to read what the poet is saying about Fortunatus, his family, and his good fortune at having so many sons.[7] A text in fragments, subject to partial readings, is drawn together as a gestalt ensemble of interrelated and mutually elaborating features; therein, the text can be read plainly for what it literally says. The discovered precision and completeness of the text offers itself and identifies it as a poetic object.

Carl Fernbach-Flarsheim's "suicide" poem (Figure 2) also offers this "miracle" of reading.[8] Through the suggestion that this poem is a contemplation of suicide, the reader finds in its title, "death poem #3," the fact that it is the third in a series, purposefully working toward something that poems #1 and #2 did not achieve. The text is a poem in progress, splattered as random letters and emendation marks upon a page, the "explosion" of the mind of the poet considering his death. The word "suicide" draws together the features of the text as a "gestalt ensemble" of reading's work. That ensemble even comments on the poetic object, hence itself, as being such an ensemble: in offering itself as something that is pointedly not a described organization for reading's work, "death poem #3" provides a precise description that that is the way it should be read.

II

In contrast to popular fiction or the newspaper, the poetic object is a specific and specifically witnessed achievement. First, the problematic and unfinished character of the text is seen. Why is it written in just this way? Then, a transformation: the reader finds the clarity of the text's expression. Through this transformation, the work of reading becomes visible. The poetic object serves as a natural incongruity experiment, revealing the traces of reading's

Figure 2

work. The reader must consciously implement the skills of reading, normalizing both text and reading within, and as, a text/reading pair.

How is the literary demonstration possible? How, by beginning with an obscure text and adding a single remark—"a sniper hunting for the enemy," "a cuckold," "a suicide note"—does a text come to reveal its self-sufficient precision of expression?

The interpretive remark, if articulated properly, shows how to begin to organize this communal work of reading. Through the remark, the reader finds how the interstices of the text provide an interface for the organization of reading's work that the remark projects. Against the background of shared reading skills, readers find the way to read the text, not for themselves individually but as the way the text itself describes and as the way our society should read it. The text is discovered as a poetic object, as a [text/reading] pair. The literary demonstration appears as a "miracle" because the witnessed poetic object trivializes the exegetical commentary and because the reader passes over the practices of reading—in their utter familiarity, ordinariness, and unremarkableness—that make the miracle come true. The poetic object emerges from the communal background of skills of reading which, at the same time, it molds to itself.

The origin of the exegetical "miracle" lies in the ordinary skills of reading as well: a text will first appear as an incoherent collection of contextual clues; a horizontal way of reading is seen which promises to fit those clues together; by re-embedding those clues within the ordinary practices of reading, the text unfolds as a naturally analyzable object, saying what it says because the ordinariness of the work of its reading is now its accomplishment. The "miracle" is the discovery of the coherence and continuity of the underlying contextual clues as a description of a method of reading.

There is a fragility to this achievement. It depends on a prior mystery of reading, on the text having been read, originally, in a different way. This mystery having been seen, like all mysteries, it becomes open to other explanations and to the claims that it should be left and appreciated as a mystery. At the same time, if the interpretive remark shows us how to begin to organize our work of reading a text, it also solicits and finds a community that can read the text as it suggests. It offers instruction in how we should read—that we should organize our reading so that the interpretive remark becomes "true," that "a sniper is hunting for the enemy." Much as we would like to say that the exegesis ultimately has nothing to do with our reading, it hovers around our reading as its organizational theme. Here, then, we also see that it is not really a "miracle"; it has our fingerprints on it.

4.

PROBLEMS OF READING

Much of reading's work is unremarkable, specifically uninteresting, and utterly ordinary. In the Owen poem, the observation that a single voice speaks the lines is trivial, as are the observations that the poem builds to a conclusion, that the speaker is listening for another person, and that their meeting bodes ill. Saying that Fortunatus is a portrait-painter and that his sons do not look like him is obvious. On the other hand, these texts present specific problems for laic reading—the reason that the speaker in Owen's poem is searching for another person, the logic of the Fortunatus text.

The literary demonstration implicitly identifies these problems of reading by offering solutions for them. Rather than describing the work of reading directly, the literary demonstration describes and analyzes the achievement of the poetic object. It describes and analyzes what the result of reading a text might be, and therein it gives tacit directions for the organization of reading's work. By addressing and solving problems of reading *simpliciter*,[1] critical reading lodges itself with ordinary reading and develops its own alchemy of reading practice. It offers the completeness that the poetic object initially lacks.

Consider one of Dylan Thomas's "Altarwise" sonnets.[2]

> First there was the lamb on knocking knees
> And three dead seasons on a climbing grave
> That Adam's wether in the flock of horns,
> Butt of the tree-tailed worm that mounted Eve,
> Horned down with skullfoot and the skull of toes
> On thunderous pavements in the garden time;
> Rip of the vaults, I took my marrow-ladle
> Out of the wrinkled undertaker's van,
> And, Rip Van Winkle from a timeless cradle,
> Dipped me breast-deep in the descended bone;
> The black ram, shuffling of the year, old winter,
> Alone alive among his mutton fold,

> We rung our weathering changes on the ladder,
> Said the antipodes, and twice spring chimed.

One reading of the first six lines of the sonnet is that it describes a scene of animal copulation: first there was a lamb (on knocking knees) and a ewe (a climbing grave that carried the lamb for three seasons)[3] that Adam's wether, with his "butt" like the "tree-tailed worm that mounted Eve," had horned down, mounting and straining with his bony hooves and his bonelike muzzle, on "thunderous pavements in the garden time." Reshaped to reflect this reading, the text might appear:

> First there was the lamb on knocking knees
> And three dead seasons on a climbing grave
>   That Adam's wether in the flock of horns,
>   Butt of the tree-tailed worm that mounted Eve,
>   Horned down with skullfoot and the skull of toes
>   On thunderous pavements in the garden time;

The lines that follow this scene give metaphorical content to it. The lamb that resulted from the mating happens "First," then an "I" speaks. Through the sequence of scenes, their juxtaposition, and the fact that the "I" is introduced through the phrase "Rip of the vaults," the "I" is read as the "lamb," seen at the present time. A parallel between the scenes is exhibited, as well as a consequential development between them: first "I" was a lamb, then:

> Rip of the vaults, I took my marrow-ladle
> Out of the wrinkled undertaker's van,
> And, Rip Van Winkle from a timeless cradle,
> Dipped me breast-deep in the descended bone;

On the level of a full-voiced, dramatic reading, the poem tells a story: first, the mating of a ram and ewe is described, in part as a metaphor for the conception of the speaker of the lines; the "lamb" is then initiated sexually; finally, there is a resolution between the aging adult and the younger man—the old and young men "ring" their "changes."

> First there was the lamb on knocking knees
> And three dead seasons on a climbing grave
> That Adam's wether in the flock of horns,
> Butt of the tree-tailed worm that mounted Eve,
> Horned down with skullfoot and the skull of toes
> On thunderous pavements in the garden time;

Rip of the vaults, I took my marrow-ladle
Out of the wrinkled undertaker's van,
And, Rip Van Winkle from a timeless cradle,
Dipped me breast-deep in the descended bone;
The black ram, shuffling of the year, old winter,
Alone alive among his mutton fold,
We rung our weathering changes on the ladder,
Said the antipodes, and twice spring chimed.

This reading works as a temporally developing, oral reading. Close inspection of the text, however, leads to problems. The description in lines 7 through 10 does not quite make sense; the order of actions seems to be reversed. One solution is to see Thomas, identifying himself with his "marrow-ladle," pulling himself out of the womb and being dipped in a world which owes itself to Adam. But how, then, is the parallel to the lamb explained, for it is a lamb who is already born and on knocking knees? The contrast becomes unclear. Moreover, once such symbolism is introduced, each image in the text is open to similar interrogation; the continuity of reading the sonnet disintegrates and becomes a puzzle. How are allusions such as "Adam's wether" integrated within such a reading, especially if a coherent scheme of meaning for these allusions is required?

William Tindall analyzes the sonnet differently:

> The metaphor of sheep, unfolding from lamb to ram, through wether, mutton, flock, and fold (cf. 174), includes Thomas' present and future conditions, the seasons, and the globe. As a child of one or two, Thomas is like the lamb of God or Jesus. His "knocking knees," which combine knock-knees with terror and knocking to get out (cf. 7, 19), remind him of his "three dead seasons" (nine months) in the "climbing grave" of the womb. (Compare "running grave," 18. "Climbing," which recalls the ladder of II, is only one of the intricate connections that link these sonnets.) But back to our muttons: "Adam's wether," who "horned" Thomas down in genetic "garden time" must be father. A wether, the ram who leads the flock, is generally, but not always, castrated. If emasculate now, like the old gentleman who lost his mandrake, father must have lost his parts by giving them to a son. The "flock of horns" is the flock he leads: horned sheep or devils perhaps, but hardly cuckolds. "Butt," combining verb and noun, the butting ram and his object, also combines and divides head and tail. This combination of opposites leads to antipodal skull and foot or death and sex. (Compare "the poles of skull and toes," 24.) If skull suggests Golgotha, the garden could also be Gethsemane; for Christ and Adam are both around. Their "thunderous pavements," through which hemlocks thrust, are laid by the short spark (II).[4]

Beneath the exegetical text, Tindall struggles with the problems of reading. Tindall understands that the imagery is of a sexual nature, and he is at pains to connect it to his reading. In the quotation above and in further remarks quoted below, he struggles as well with the use of the word "wether." At least in common usage, a wether is a sheep castrated before maturity; twist as one will, a wether will not have progeny. Arguably, Thomas needed synonyms, and "Adam's wether" fits the intonation and cadence of the lines that the word itself helps to create.

Tindall does not describe his reading of the sonnet directly; he treats it as if it can be assumed. His critical text is an analysis of that reading. The reader must see through Tindall's analysis to find the reading that Tindall proposes, and the reader must have the skills of reading that are required to do this. Tindall, however, does offer a reading of the opening of the sonnet: first there was the lamb (on knocking knees, after having spent three dead seasons in the womb) that Adam's wether genetically horned down through the ages (as Adam genetically "horned" us down) in the garden time of creation. Thus, the text is read as follows:

> First there was the lamb
> on knocking knees and three dead seasons on a
> climbing grave
> That Adam's wether in the flock of horns,
> Butt of the tree-tailed worm that mounted Eve,
> Horned down with skullfoot and the skull of toes
> On thunderous pavements in the garden time;

This reading is imbued with difficulties. If Thomas is the one who was horned down and is now only one year old, the seventh through tenth lines of the poem lose their descriptiveness of sexual intercourse; they become metaphoric and allegorical. Tindall recognizes the problem and tries to make sense of it. In fact, as seen below, he reverses the order of lines as a means of resolving the problem; he reads the lines

> And, Rip Van Winkle from a timeless cradle,
> Dipped me breast-deep in the descended bone . . .

before those of

> Rip of the vaults, I took my marrow-ladle
> Out of the wrinkled undertaker's van . . .

There is nothing essentially wrong in this. Tindall is attempting to describe a gestalt of reading practice which may be more easily explained and taught through such a transposition. Making the alteration explicit, however, allows the reader to examine the practices of reading the text to see if the text provides the grounds for such a reversal. More important, given the structure of reading that Tindall has described for the first ten lines, the last four become a very serious muddle:

> Adam and Christ, falling and rising, lead to Rip Van Winkle, sleeping and waking, like Finnegan [of *Finnegans Wake*]. Like this earlier Rip, young Thomas wakes from sleep in the "timeless cradle" of the womb, where he has dipped in the "descended bone" of death and sex. There or here, as "Rip of the vaults," he is lord of tomb and womb. In short, as we already know, he is alive and something of a rip. "I took my marrow-ladle / Out of the wrinkled undertaker's van" is one of Thomas' most wonderful pictures, surrealist in all but rational control. That the van is ripped and wrinkled adds to the fun. Translated, the "undertaker's van" is only the womb, and the "marrow-ladle" is only what serves life and dishes it. But the picture, greater than the translation, is diminished by it. Better to enjoy manifest wonders without laying them on the couch.
> Rip brings ram back to mind by sound. Starting as white lamb, Thomas will grow to be the black "ram rod" of "Lament," the only one who is not cold mutton in a flock of muttonheads, a ram among the ninnies, and "the black spit of the chapel fold" (174). But ram unites this butting future with an innocent present. Spring lamb becomes ram of spring. As a sign of the zodiac, the Ram ushers in the poet's spring as old winter shuffles off. (The sense is clearer than the syntax here.) As unemasculated wether, Thomas the ram, young or old, is a bellwether, leading the flock and boss of the fold. The ladder of the wether's weathers rings because it has rungs. The antipodes, which bring us back to the globe of the first sonnet and the poles of skull and foot, ring spring out twice, like a clock—an ambiguous clock; for ringing twice could mean either that the child is now two years old or one. The sun, moving between Capricorn and Cancer, brings the world two springs a year. If young Thomas is the whole world, he is one year old. If only a hemisphere, like someone in Plato, Thomas is two.[5]

If the first lines of the poem are read as Tindall suggests—that Adam's wether genetically horned down Thomas the lamb—the symbolic references of the poem take on larger significance. If Thomas is one year old in this sonnet as part of a reading of the "Altarwise" sequence as a whole, what can be made of Thomas's marrow-ladle activities? The precise descriptive sense of the lines is problematic in any case. And if the sonnet is read in the manner that Tindall intends, the last lines do present a muddle which needs to be explained.

Whichever of the two analyses is preferred, their juxtaposition shows, in fact, that they are both dealing with very similar problems of reading. The sentence structure of the first six lines of the sonnet is ambiguous: does Adam's wether horn down the lamb with "knocking knees / And three dead seasons on a climbing grave," or does it horn down "three dead seasons on a climbing grave"? The resolution of this ambiguity depends on two aspects of reading the text: the meaning of "three dead seasons on a climbing grave" and whether "the lamb" has, as its properties, both knocking knees and three dead seasons.

Both readings give definiteness to these phrases as a solution to the problems of reading that underlie them. Both readings identify "the lamb" as the speaker of the lines and as having metaphoric significance for that speaker. This is tied to a prior achievement of reading's work: the sonnet has a tripartite structure, reflected in its three main clauses—a first scene (lines 1–6) which is introduced as a "First" of something; a juxtaposed scene (lines 7–10) which creates dramatic tension and introduces the subject "I" which the first scene then appears to concern; and a final scene (lines 11–14) which offers some form of resolution. However, the nature of the conflict and that of its resolution are not clear. Both readings provide formulations of that conflict and resolution, thereby providing directions for organizing the work of reading to recover a sense of those formulations in a reading of the text.

Each of the readings elucidates features of the text that are essential to the promised demonstration. In one reading, the word "the" in "the lamb" is unstressed; in Tindall's reading, "the" gains relevance as "the lamb of God." In the first reading, a scheme of references is used to exhibit the real-worldly descriptiveness of the sonnet; in the second, the symbolism of the text is emphasized, and problems of reading are articulated and solved through it. The imagery in the poem lacks definiteness, and both readings attempt to provide a coherent scheme of meaning for it. Both readings also identify Thomas as the speaker of the lines, based on the tone of the poem as speaking directly about the world.

These readings are similar in another way. Both attempt to provide a literal reading of the text: they attempt to show how Thomas's poem can actually be read. "Reading-really," "reading literally," and "literal reading" refer to the recovery of a text's reading from within the activity of reading itself, whether that reading involves figurative language or symbolism, metaphysical meaning or self-reflective analysis. "Reading-really," "reading literally," and "literal reading" concern the detailed work of reading an always specific text.

When Elder Olson analyzes the symbolism in Dylan Thomas's poetry, he is attempting to show how this poetry can be read literally to recover the concreteness of its images, metaphors, and symbols. He is teaching a method of reading Thomas literally.[6]

Here is the fetus in the womb:

> In the groin of the natural doorway I crouched like a tailor
> Sewing a shroud for a journey. . . .[7]

Here is the child at the moment of birth:

> . . . I rush in a crouch the ghost with a hammer, air. . . .[8]

Here is the mysterious interior geography of the body:

> Dawn breaks behind the eyes;
> From poles of skull and toe the windy blood
> Slides like a sea. . . .[9]

Literary criticism is about reading-really and offers itself as a pedagogy of reading.

If there is a difference between our own and Tindall's reading, it lies in the conception of reading-really. The first reading seeks to reveal a self-sustaining, naturally analyzable reading of the sonnet—an analyzability that is embedded in the ordinary skills of reading, an analyzability through which the adequacies and inadequacies of the text-as-read are inspectable as the work of reading. Tindall's reading references the critical community for which his reading, in itself, is an exhibition of the arts and analyzability of reading.

The artifactual texts that result from these two approaches to, and meanings of, "reading" are different: for one, a naturally analyzable text is revealed; for the other, a text which exhibits the reasons and motives for its being read in a certain way.

5.

THE NATURALLY ANALYZABLE TEXT

Many of us have made a telephone call to a "friend," one with whom we speak regularly, which began something like this:

—Hello.
—Hello, Tom?
—Yes?
—Uh, this is Eric.
—Yes?

When Tom says "Hello," we hear that it is Tom, and when we say "Hello, Tom?" we use the reasonableness of the question to announce who we are. The response that we might expect is "Eric?" or "Eric, is that you?" or "Eric, how ar'ya?" Tom's first "Yes?" is ambiguous: it may indicate that he does not recognize the voice, or it could mean "something else." Our reply—"Uh, this is Eric"—attempts to repair this ambiguity. The situation becomes clear with Tom's second "Yes?"

When we call people on the telephone, we are summoning them to the phone.[1] Because we are summoning them, we are expected to have some type of news to tell—a reason for the call—even if it is only the news that we want to talk. Tom's second "Yes?" demands that an explicit reason be stated immediately. At the same time, by doing this, Tom also clarifies his first "Yes?" He did recognize the caller; he just does not want to speak to that person very much: "If you are calling me, Eric, you need a reason; just tell me that reason; I'm not up to pleasantries right now, at least not with the likes of you!"

The actual words of the conversation do not necessarily exhibit this analysis. There are other reasons for saying the same words; in a different context, they might have a different meaning or show a different intention. Those of us, however, who have made such calls or have answered a telephone in this way know that "something" very close to this analysis is at issue. The analysis of the different utterances is not the disengaged, objective analysis of a scientist; instead, the analyzability of the conversation is already part of the conversation. Answering Tom's first "Yes?" with "Uh, this is Eric" is an attempt to clarify what Tom could be heard to be asking, and Tom's second "Yes?" is a corrective to that attempt at mishearing. The telephone conversation is naturally analyzable: its analyzability is already embedded in the conversation; it is embedded in the conversation through the ways in which the conversation is produced, and it must be embedded in a conversation for that conversation to be organized, produced, and continued as that particular telephone conversation.[2]

The poetic object is not, initially, a naturally analyzable object. It first appears as something different from an ordinary text; its promised achievement is a reorganization of the skills of reading from within which the reading of its text will be evident. In contrast to the telephone conversation, reading a poetic object's text is similar to walking down a sidewalk with a friend and finding oneself on the grass, heading for the curb. Readers try to normalize the text by embedding it within the ordinary practices of reading. Put differently, readers try to develop a method of reading that recovers the text as a naturally analyzable object.

I

Often the word "method" is used to refer to an abstract procedure—for example, the scientific, accountable methods for conducting chemistry experiments or the methods for properly selecting people for a survey. The word "method," however, has a humble, "improper" counterpart that official methods frequently try to repair. How we adjust and maintain social distance provides an example of such ordinary methods, as do the methods through which we prepare and cook dinner. If we move to a new apartment, we find that we have to re-embed and habituate our cooking methods into the new kitchen.

As an accessible example, consider how we go about adding up a column of numbers such as the one below.

$$
\begin{array}{r}
23 \\
45 \\
49 \\
11 \\
87 \\
35 \\
14 \\
23 \\
19 \\
\hline
\end{array}
$$

Let us begin not with what people say about columnar addition but by examining their actual arithmetic practices. Although not everyone does columnar arithmetic exactly in the manner that will be described, practical adders do these "sorts of things"; they do them when they add; and what follows is a description of the types of things that they do.

We begin at the top of the right column with every intention of working sequentially from top to bottom and, therein, keeping our place in the calculation and doing it "properly." Adding 3 and 5, we get 8. But then we see that adding 9 and 1 gives 10 (Figure 3). Adding 10 and 8 is easy—we "replace" the 0 in the 10 with 8 and "say" (perhaps quite literally) 18, at the same time that we move our pencil so that it is now positioned on the 7. The 8 in the 18 and the 7 make 15, and 15 and 10 make 25, so we have 25; then we add 5 to get 30. Adding 4 to 30 is easy; having just "said" 30, we now "say" 34. This much at least has been straightforward. Now we get busy: 3 is just 3 and it is a lot easier simply to tap 3 out with our pencil, counting as we go, the tapping keeping a mechanical rhythm to allow us to remember that we give just three counts: 35, 36, 37. Figure 4 has been marked with three dots to indicate this process.

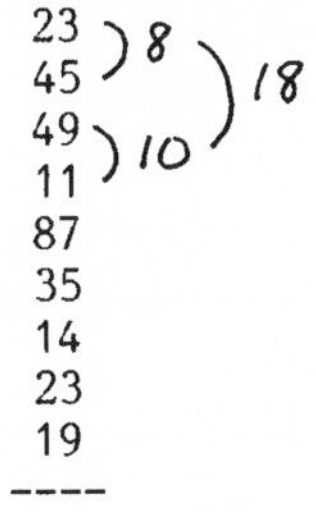

Figure 3 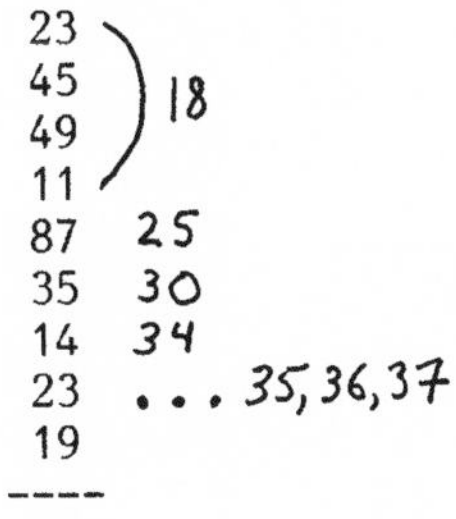   Figure 4 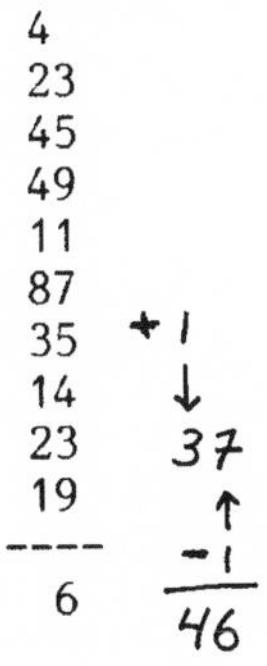   Figure 5

The sum to this point is 37, and the next number to add is 9. When adding 9 to a number, we know that the one's digit in that number goes down one— so the 7 in 37 goes to 6—and the digit in the ten's place goes up one, from 3 to 4. So we have 6 and a carry of 4, which we write at the top of the column on the left (Figure 5).

We turn now to the second column. 4 and 2 and 4 make 10; and the next 4 and 1 make 5, so we have 15 (Figure 6). We next see that the 8 and 2 make 10—that is, we look for 10s or for other easy additions (Figure 7). We now have 25. Perhaps marking this pairing, or crossing out the numbers to help keep our place in the sum, we then begin tapping again: 26, 27, 28 (for the 3 following the 8), 29 (for the 1 following the 3), and then, skipping the 2, 30 (for the final 1) (Figure 8).

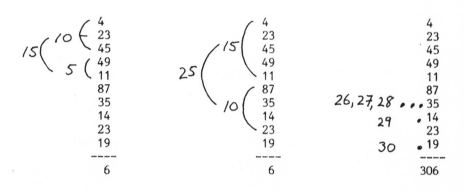

Figure 6   Figure 7   Figure 8

This description gives a sense of columnar arithmetic as an ongoing activity. Once the description of the calculation is understood for what it illuminates, we realize that we do columnar addition using very similar, if not identical, practical devices. The details of the process are extremely fine, as, for example, the question of when and how, from within the course of this process, the practical need for these circumstantial methods arises. Nothing is particularly hidden about the process; we all know how to do such calculations and use similar practical methods to accomplish them. Rather than being foreign or exotic, the process that has been described, if not precise, is familiar, obvious, and transparent. Generally, these methods are not attended to in a thematic manner, especially by the person engaged in the addition, who simply wishes to complete the sum. We discount these methods; they seem to involve our own personal idiosyncrasies; they may even embarrass us.

Although the particulars of such practical computational methods may differ between individuals, a few properties of such calculations in general can be listed:

- Columnar arithmetic involves local, circumstantially developing methods for adding up such sums; faced with such a sum, the practical adder figures out a way of doing the calculation, and figures out that procedure as he or she is doing the calculation.

- That the numbers are being added up properly is tied to the local, circumstantially developing methods that the practical adder is using for adding them up.

- When and if practical adders lose their place in such an addition, they are really losing their place in the circumstantially developing methods that are being used to get the addition done.

- That the addition appears to be correct in the midst of the calculation is not a consequence of the abstract, mathematical properties of numbers, or of accounts about how such calculations are done properly, but of the properties of numbers as they appear from within the course of the "improper" work of their summation.

- If the practical adder tries to avoid such "irregular" methods—attempting, for example, to add each number to the next systematically from top to bottom—the addition becomes more difficult: with each new number, the adder has to remember the addition table—"what is 25 plus 7?"— and therein the practical adder begins to be distracted.[3]

Like practical addition, reading also consists of circumstantially developing methods of getting the work of reading done. These methods assure readers that they are reading correctly; when something goes wrong, they inspect the text as a means of inspecting their, and the society's, practices of reading. Like the phenomenology of arithmetic, the activity of reading is always there for anyone to see, in and as our own practices of reading. Reading's work is not hidden, but familiar and in plain sight. Like columnar addition, however, reading is also subject to a peculiar mystification. The detailed work of reading is seen but passed over in favor of its transcendentalizing achievement.

In the addition problem, the sum itself does not ensure the adequacy of the addition. There is no way of looking at the number 306 to see if it is correct. Nor by repeating the calculations with a calculator or a computer can we be sure of its accuracy.[4] Hidden within our own practices of doing the calculation, there may be something that we are doing wrong, but doing it quite consistently. People who have been hypnotized to count to 10 leaving out 7 may repeatedly grasp their fingers and call out numbers—1, 2, 3, 4, 5, 6, 8, 9, 10—but they are left with an extra finger.[5] No matter how carefully the process is monitored, an extra finger always remains. The person is in a real quandary over how this could possibly be. Similarly, the practical adder may repeatedly check the calculations, attending ever more carefully to the way that the calculation is being done or applying different, but equally unavoidable, practical methods to do the sum some other way.[6] The idea of a "correct sum" identifies the project and informs the work of its completion; that the resulting sum is "correct" is assured only through the practices of adding up the numbers.

Reading is directed toward what the text "says." While the organization of our work of reading is guided by and uses the linear temporality of reading line by line, left to right, down the page, the continuity and coherence of our organization of reading's work resides in its achievement. We rush to the end of the mystery novel to see why the author has involved us in just this course of reading. Reading always aims at its own transcendentalizing achievement—the discovery and unfolding of a text/reading pair.

A poetic object problematizes such action; in fact, it needs to do this in order to be a discovery concerning the arts of reading. The poetic object organizes text and reading as an original [text/reading] pair. The practical adder seeks a method of performing a calculation; the reader searches the text to find a way of reading it. The reader seeks a method of reading that re-embeds the text within reading's ordinary, laic work. In the process, the text becomes available as a naturally analyzable text, available to be read by anyone who can read competently.

II

Sometimes poems are presented as objects divorced from their reading, for which the poetry of e. e. cummings seems to be a favored example. Students are told that poetry is writing with white space on the right instead of a solid margin. They are asked to look at poems as if they were paintings and, specifically, as texts which are not yet read.

Oddly, the point that is being made is the opposite of what it first appears to be: poetry is not poetry because it sounds or appears as poetry "should"; it is not a text divorced from the activity of reading that animates it. Imagining that students think that poems should sound and look like greeting card poesy is a convenient fiction. By using this fiction, the instructor avoids having to articulate what is poetic about a poetic text.[7]

Poetry is poetry not because of the shape or the sound of the words, but because the words and sounds fit together as a distinctive and original poetic object. The idiosyncrasy of the poetic object seems to disallow its general characterization. But how, unless we really want to look at a poem as a docent looks at a painting in a museum, do we find a method of reading a poem that recovers its distinctive particularity as such an object?

The opening stanza of T. S. Eliot's *The Waste Land* provides an occasion for examining this process, and a method of reading will be developed that makes the stanza available to reading *simpliciter*. The actual text of *The Waste Land* should be at hand here and throughout the rest of this book. Here, the text needs to be consulted to see that the stanza can, in fact, be read in the manner described. Later, critical writings on the same stanza will be examined, and the text will need to be examined to see, in detail, how the stanza is being read by the literary critic, what the process of "reading" becomes and, therein, to what the activity of "reading" refers for the critical community.

Let us begin with the text of *The Waste Land* before us. It opens with a quotation from Petronius: the Cumaean Sibyl, given longevity by Apollo but not permanent youth, is now ancient, shriveled, hanging in a jar; as part of the actual quotation, when asked what she wants, she says that she wants to die.[8] Then follows the dedication to Ezra Pound. The body of *The Waste Land* proper is divided into five parts, the first of which is entitled "The Burial of the Dead." We wish to concentrate on the opening stanza of this first part.

The title "The Burial of the Dead" is strange, for who else, if not the dead, are to be buried? In a sense, the title is a promise. We "pass beyond" the title and look to the text to explicate its particular meaning and emphasis. Similarly, that the first stanza is a coherent "unit" within the poem might be seen as a promise. Visually, prosodically, substantively, and narratively, the second stanza is different from the first. But, like the title, this division is a question, something that must be substantiated in and through a reading of the poem. At the same time, in observing these aspects of the text, we have already started to find particular relevances for our work of reading.

The cultivation of an accountable reading of the opening stanza might begin with the examination of the first four lines.

> April is the cruellest month, breeding
> Lilacs out of the dead land, mixing
> Memory and desire, stirring
> Dull roots with spring rain.

There are at least two ways of reading these lines. Whoever is speaking them could be saying them as matters of fact, as a principled description—April is the type of thing which is cruel; it causes lilacs to breed; dull roots are stirred to life. This stresses the assertive character of the lines. The lines could also be read as revealing the psychology of the person who says or thinks them: since April itself is not "cruel" and does not "breed" lilacs, such statements reflect personal perceptions. The person who is "saying" the lines thinks of spring in this way.

Following the opening lines of the poem, the pronoun "us" is introduced. In these lines (5–7), the comparative virtues of winter are described—its warmth, the forgetfulness of snow. The "us" that appears is a general "us"—winter kept all of "us" warm. Nevertheless, even though a general "us," the pronoun personalizes the speaker; retrospectively we understand the speaker of the preceding lines as one of "us," and therefore as one for whom April is cruel. In this way, we have begun to organize our work of reading this stanza so as to find the presence of a speaker whose utterances reflect that particular person's feelings. We have begun to build a method for reading the text.

What do the first four lines tell us about this speaker? The lines can be read to say that April is cruel, for the person saying the lines, because April breeds, because it mixes, because it stirs. "Breeding" is normally used to describe the mating of animals, not the natural germination and flowering of plants. We notice the strange usage. We notice, as well, the emphasis on "dead." Land, of course, is inanimate, neither "dead" nor "alive." The word points to the barrenness of the land, but gives that barrenness a slightly different emphasis. The following paraphrase offers itself: the speaker of the lines sees, in the flowering of spring, animalistic breeding; this recalls memories, and particularly memories of desire; it is his or her "dull roots"—those of memory and desire—that are "stirring."

That the opening lines of The Waste Land can be read or "understood" in this way is already a reference to an organization of the work of reading such that this can be said about them. This "understanding" reflects the commonality of the skills of reading. Ordinary readers can read the lines in this way, and therein the lines, in turn, come to evidence just this way of reading. From within the work of reading, the words take on their collective meaning, and that meaning is equivalent to the organization of the work of reading of which the words and their meanings are a part.

As elementary, provisional, and prospective as these first observations may be, they can be used to continue and perpetuate the organization of reading's work in which the observations are already embedded. Following the first four lines, the past tense of line 5 claiming the warmth of winter tells us not only that the previous description of April is a reflection of the emotions of the person who "says" them, but that April is the present time of the speaker's utterances; the speaker is reacting to this new spring. Lines 5–7 use the same technique as the first four lines: they convey the attitude of their speaker, not through explicit statement but through the description that the speaker gives of the past winter. Snow is not "forgetful," nor does winter give warmth. A contrast is being made: if April is cruel for recalling memories and desires, winter was better for allowing the speaker to forget and to live on, if in a meager way.

Putting these lines together with the next four (lines 8–11), the reader follows the "speaker" of the lines back in time: beginning with the painfulness of the new (and possibly metaphorical) spring, regretting the passing of the metaphorical winter when memories and desires were forgotten, the speaker recalls a specific summer further in the past. The specificity of the summer setting and the fact that a "we" waited for a shower to pass and had coffee together evidence the passage as the memory of particular events and particular people. The "us" is no longer a general "us"; it refers to the speaker of the lines and some other person or people, a definite "we." The summer passage is in the past tense; the ease of its description and its lack of somberness tell us that it is further in the past. From spring to winter to some earlier summer, the speaker has gone back in time. Since the speaker has already indicated a desire not to remember something—the developing organization of our work of reading being the grounds for saying this—the reader understands this new setting as part of that which was to be avoided, thereby maintaining and extending that organization.

Following the line

> And drank coffee, and talked for an hour.

line 12 of the poem is in German. Roughly translated, it says "not Russian, from Lithuania, [I'm] real [or genuine] German." The grammatical construction indicates that it is spoken by a woman. If people are in the Hofgarten drinking coffee and talking, there is some chance that they will be speaking German; in fact, there is some chance that the quoted line belonged to their conversation. The construction directly preceding the line in German—that some "we" "talked for an hour"—offers further grounds for such a reading. Because line 11 ends abruptly with the statement that the people "talked for an hour," the next line appears, in its natural analyzability within a course of reading that is simultaneously being developed through that construction, as part of that conversation: we talked for an hour, and this is one thing that was said. The line itself, rendering conversational speech rather than literary usage, is that of a "patriotic" German, a woman claiming that she is real, in the sense of genuine, German. I have been told by native speakers that it is blunt and assertive, and that the sentiment expressed is distasteful.[9]

Now, however, we have a puzzle. If the speaker of the stanza is recalling something from the past that he or she does not want to remember, and recalls this particular line of conversation from those happier times, what does this line (or the sentiment that it expresses) have to do with the painfulness of the memories? Or with anything else?

The text continues:

> And when we were children, staying at the archduke's,
> My cousin's, he took me out on a sled,
> And I was frightened. He said, Marie,
> . . .

The reader needs to attend to the grammatical structure of this passage. When the "we" of the lines were children, they stayed at the residence of the archduke, which is the same as "My cousin's." The "he" who took "me" on a sled ride is not the archduke but one of the "we" who were children together. The lines, however, tell us more. The nonspecific "we" of the Hofgarten is Marie and a man who, as a child, took Marie on the sled ride. Through the device of having the speaker retell what this other child said, the reader learns—or reads—that the person actually speaking (or thinking) the lines of the text is Marie. It is Marie who regrets the coming of spring and the memories that it has occasioned, who preferred the forgetfulness of winter, who remembers the events in the Hofgarten and the sled ride.

Following the description of the sled ride, the stanza concludes with the lines

> In the mountains, there you feel free.
> I read, much of the night, and go south in the winter.

The line "In the mountains, there you feel free" is read as a comment on the sled episode. The "you" is not read as a general "you," but as Marie speaking about Marie; Marie felt free in the mountains. However, as soon as she has recalled the sled ride, Marie distances herself from it—both in time of day and in place. The relevance of "much of the night" is not yet clear, but the reader does understand that the "he" of the sled ride is no longer present: "I," Marie, is the one who now, in the present, does these things.

If this is it, if this is the sense that can be made of reading the stanza, what does the agonizing about April, memories, and desires in the first lines concern? A time of childhood excitement? Here, then, like the line in German, is another puzzle. Both are puzzles of and for reading; to examine them, we need to articulate more finely the work of reading the text.

Let us consider the sled episode more closely. Although told about children, the episode can be read as a premonition and, now that it is in memory, as a re-enactment of a sexual relationship. Let us suppose that Marie and this man with whom she was in the Hofgarten were lovers. The sled adventure, in its pacing and content, embodies and figuratively re-enacts the sexuality of their relationship. When Marie says that she reads at night and goes south in the winter, she is distancing herself both from the real time (night) and from the real or figurative place (the mountains) of their lovemaking.

> And when we were children, staying at the archduke's,
> My cousin's, he took me out on a sled,
> And I was frightened. He said, Marie,
> Marie, hold on tight. And down we went.
> In the mountains, there you feel free.

Now, however, Marie is alone. Her lover is no longer present; she reads at night; she journeys south in the winter, away from the snowy mountains. We are not told explicitly why this is so. Where has the other person gone?

The relevance of the line in German and of the title "The Burial of the Dead" now becomes clearer. As the woman of the pair in the Hofgarten having the conversation, Marie herself is the one who proclaims her true Germanness. The new spring has brought back memories of Marie's past; in particular, she remembers herself exhibiting her chauvinism to her lover who, as a young man associated with the aristocracy, might well have fought and been killed in World War I. Therein, we begin to see the painful remembrances that Marie has; in the memories that April has brought, she is now, in fact, enacting a "burial of the dead."

This is Marie's "story." Marie, the "speaker" of the lines, rues the coming of spring and the memories that it occasions. She remembers a time spent with a lover: caught in a summer shower, they waited for it to pass, and had coffee and talked. Then, the disturbing recollection of pride in German origins, followed by the recollection of the sensuality of her relationship with a man now dead. Now, alone, she simply goes on living.

Marie is not telling us her story with little clues that we must piece together. The text has been constructed so that she is recalling her own memories and reacting to them. What she "says" or "thinks" is not for us but from her own perspective; she need not identify for herself whom or what she is addressing. Eliot has left enough detail for the reader to find, in Marie's utterances, the underlying story that is being told. The first stanza should be read as a continuous whole to see that it can, in fact, be read quite literally in this manner, that the voicing of the lines becomes clear, and that the lines of the text fit together to form a coherent unit.

In contrast and as commentary on this first stanza, the narrator of the opening of the second stanza of "The Burial of the Dead" has a radically different "voice." The second stanza begins with the rhetorical question of a biblical prophet, at once asking, metaphorically, what makes up the waste land we know as the world, and at the same time by so asking, offering and proclaiming the present world as such a metaphor. Addressing the listener as a "Son of man," the voice tells such listeners that they cannot even guess at an answer, because of the desolate landscape they know as their world.

Given the difference between this voice and the voice of the previous stanza, the first stanza is appreciated retrospectively as a coherent whole. Marie's experiences are the experiences of one of the people of "the waste land." It is just one of many such experiences of the present world for which the opening voice of the second stanza then provides commentary: there is something even worse than death running to catch up to us in youth or than death looming ahead as we get older (see lines 28–29); nothing in the end awaits, only that we are turned to dust. The prophet promises:

> I will show you fear in a handful of dust.

This, too, is a voice from, and of, the waste land.

By problematizing the work of reading, the opening of *The Waste Land* forces us to explicate that work. We develop a method of reading that embeds the text in reading's ordinary work. The achievement of that method is the discovered, pellucid text, a coherent whole, the revealed poetic object. The achievement makes the analysis unnecessary; the text itself, embedded in the naturally analyzable work of its reading, becomes a deeply inspectable text. The fine details of the text can be consulted to see, and in turn reveal, how they describe exactly how the text should be read. When we are done, we need not remember the analysis; the analysis appears as an articulation of the ordinary work of reading, demonstrably so in that the text can now be read in just this way. It has become a naturally analyzable text, and it is a naturally analyzable text because it has been embedded in the ordinary, naturally analyzable skills of reading.

III

At each turn, the reading of the opening of *The Waste Land* did not rely on expert knowledge but on the laic skills of ordinary reading. In our working through the text, those skills were cultivated and arranged. As the accomplishment both of those skills and of our organization of them, the reading that has been found has a transcendental, objective presence—the text seems to require that it be read in this particular way. The skills of lay reading, having been so cultivated, appear as the guarantor of just this way of reading, just as we might hold our fingers and count to ten. What else could the text be read to say other than what it literally is read as saying? What else is the text, other than this naturally analyzable object?

A number of critical commentaries on the opening stanza of *The Waste Land* are presented below. We will want to examine such commentaries for the type of reading that underlies them. For the moment, however, let us view them as snapshots taken from a different culture, the first view of a terrain which we eventually seek to explore.

> The first section of "The Burial of the Dead" develops the theme of the attractiveness of death, or of the difficulty in rousing oneself from the death in life in which the people of the waste land live. Men are afraid to live in reality. April, the month of rebirth, is not the most joyful season but the cruelest. Winter at least kept us warm in forgetful snow. The idea is one which Eliot has stressed elsewhere. . . . Men dislike to be roused from their death-in-life.
> The first part of "The Burial of the Dead" introduces this theme through a sort of reverie on the part of the protagonist—a reverie in which speculation on life glides off into memory of an actual conversation in the Hofgarten and back into speculation again. The function of the conversation is to establish the class and character of the protagonist.[10]

> Who speaks the first seven lines? How persuasive are we meant to find them? And who speaks the next four, and the line in German? And who is the final speaker, this Marie who begins talking as if she needed no introduction?
> No poem before ever started so, with an "overhear me," then an "overhear *me*," and the same again, and all the while a "never mind who, for it scarcely matters anyway."
> It *is* going to matter who, and quite soon, but first the poem registers a crisis of heteroglossia, and, beyond that, a crisis of meaningless identity.[11]

> Nature awakens to new life and fertility in its eternal cycle; the "shoures swete" hailed by Chaucer have come. But there is no glad welcome to the spring. The poet's feelings towards both winter and April, towards the sus-

pension of life in which he is living, and towards a rebirth, is ambivalent, "mixing memory and desire." One impulse of both memory and desire is towards the apathy and oblivion of winter. The possibility of renewal, the thought of being stirred into potency and growth, the compulsion towards it felt in the rhythm of the first four lines, are mated and mingled with a fear and reluctance which drive him back to safe forgetfulness. Then, without transition, there is a sudden change to a rhythm of release and lightness. It is an escape, but into what? Into a world where seasons are only a matter of scenery and sports and travel, of rain and sunlight on mountain or valley, of the light superficial chatter of rootless, cosmopolitan tourists, rolling stones who are no part of the rhythm of the life-cycle. These are some of the inhabitants of the Waste Land.[12]

By these allusions implicit in April's cruelty, Eliot links Christ and Adonis to suggest that both their deaths were part of those ritual celebrations that protected man from the overwhelming power of evil. And since Adonis was a vegetative deity it is inevitable that his departure should be matched by a "dead land" filled only with "dull roots" and "dried tubers."

. . .

The "dull roots" are a vegetative analogue to human history and myth; both stretch back into "the abysm of time" which Eliot found illuminated by *The Golden Bough*. The ironic human equivalent to the "little life" of "dull roots" and "dried tubers" is found in the line: "I read, much of the night, and go south in the winter." Going south in the winter is an unconscious mimicry of the death and disappearance of the god. It is the physical, not the symbolic and spiritual, warmth of spring and summer that is sought. At the same time this endeavor to maintain perpetually the season of life and growth constitutes an implicit denial of the cyclic order of existence.[13]

As we read on we come to still a third discourse in the paragraph, not counting the wild-card line in German, namely Marie's monologue, and here we are made aware of, made to hear, metastases within a single, and fairly ordinary, discourse. We see that the few lines of narrative reminiscence—those of the second discourse—are intended to set the stage for this third one, though not merely intended for that, and that the first two discourses, if related to one another, are in themselves coherent compared to Marie's artless broken monologue, to leave aside the art that the protagonist, or Eliot, used to fake it.[14]

Part I of Eliot's *The Waste Land*[15] derives its title from the majestic Anglican service for the burial of the dead. The theme of resurrection, proclaimed through Saint Paul's subtly moving assurance that "the dead shall be raised incorruptible, and we shall be changed," finds here its counterpoint in the rhythmic annual return of spring, when once more "the cruelest month" of April touches "dull roots," and memory and desire blend an old man's inert longing and lost fulfilment.[16] Tiresias, who is speaking, has been content to let winter cover him "in forgetful snow, feeding / A little life with dried tubers." In the lines of James Thomson which Eliot put to use: "Our Mother feedeth thus our little life, / That we in turn may feed her with our death."[17] Blind and spiritually embittered, Tiresias wrestles with buried emotions unwittingly revived. In his mind "the floors of memory," as in "Rhapsody on a Windy Night," are dissolved. He is borne in phantasmagoria to scenes recalling the "Dixi, custodiam" of the rites of burial. They are scenes both of joy and of agony, and in memory they reveal that consciousness is death and that truly the speaker was alive only when he could forget. The death of winter and the life of spring usurp each other.

Memory takes him from the general truth to a particular event, to another springtime, in his youth, when warm days of the resurrection season brought rain, the water of life, with sunlight, and he was beside the Starnbergersee near the city of Munich.[18] A voice of a Lithuanian girl who recounted a childhood experience of terror, exhilaration, and freedom comes back to him. Against the double happiness of her memory and his, he must now set the present reality of the loveless, arid desert within him. He thinks of Ezekiel, the "son of man," chosen to turn the Israelites in their captivity back to God, and hence of Christ, the "Son of man," whose temples, like his own, are now in ruins. In this waste land Tiresias is the Fisher King, a type of all mighty who are fallen. . . .[19]

6.

ORDER TERMS
AND COMPETENT SYSTEMS

Traditionally, "order terms"—for example, the terms of grammatical and rhetorical analysis such as "tense" and "metaphor"—have been used in literary criticism to describe the natural orderlinesses of reading's work.[1] Order terms point to the existence of reading's work, to the self-sustaining character of that work, and to the enormous size of the domain of phenomena encompassed by that work. They also reflect the commitment of literary criticism to study the actual work of reading—to study "reading-really," not imagined or hypothetical versions of it. Order terms reveal how the work of reading is known to the critical community, and they reveal the technologies that are used in that community for its examination.

As their name suggests, order terms are descriptions of identifiable and regular patterns of reading. Used descriptively, they embody the same ambiguity found in any description of reading. Descriptions of reading unavoidably serve, at one and the same time, both as descriptions of reading and as instructions for reading. The characterization of the opening of *The Waste Land* as "paradoxical" or as "oracular in tone" invites the reader to find, through reading the text, how this is so. If Fortunatus is described as a cuckold and his name is said to be ironic, the reader can use these characterizations as a pedagogy for finding the organization of reading's work of which they speak. This ambiguity of description and instruction is built within critical reading as an intrinsic part of its alchemy of reading.

Order terms incorporate this ambiguity. They are, however, different from individual, idiosyncratic descriptions in that they are part of and constitute competent systems of analysis—again, as do the terms of grammatical and rhetorical analysis.

In the last chapter, a "museum of criticism" gathered together a number of critical commentaries on the opening of *The Waste Land*. Beneath and between these commentaries lies "reading *cultura*"—a type of reading at once different from, but also an alchemy of, the practices of ordinary reading.[2] The deeply reasoned texts discovered through reading *cultura* are achievements of reading *cultura*. The relationship between the orderlinesses of reading's work and the analytic systems involved in the use of order terms provides the background for seeing these achievements as achievements and for seeing how these achievements are produced.

I

Consider two different characterizations of the same set of actions. In one, a person is described as being a perfectionist, berating his or her colleagues, being emotionally cold, and having rigid moral standards. In the other, the same person is described as enjoying his or her work; colleagues are presented as resenting his or her abilities and dedication; the "coldness" and "moral rectitude" that the person exhibits are seen as that person's way of normalizing the hostility which he or she is actually experiencing.

From the first description, the actions of the person might be seen as symptoms of a "compulsive personality disorder"; from the second, the person may need only to develop alternative ways of dealing with an unfortunate situation. At the same time, we know that such gross characterizations are manufactured; they miss the nuances of life, and they miss the purposes for which such characterizations are offered.

For the psychoanalyst, events outside the therapeutic hour are not available for inspection, nor would they necessarily be clarifying. The phenomena to be analyzed are as certainly in the analyst's office as anywhere else. The warrant and legitimacy of a diagnosis of a "compulsive personality disorder," for example, depends, among other aspects of an analysis, on the patient's attempts, within the therapy, to rigidly organize the patient-analyst interactions, to continually assess the usefulness of the discussion, to engage in excessive rationalizations, to insist on the duties and obligations of the analyst, yet to be indecisive on questions regarding the patient's own personal preferences. Only by reference to the patient's efforts at orchestrating the patient-analyst interactions does the analyst see such "symptoms" as symptoms and see how they fit together as an underlying personality disorder.

Lying beneath and supporting the theories and technical terminology of psychoanalysis, the interpersonal character of the therapeutic encounter is the heart of an analysis, and it is to this that the psychoanalyst directs his or her attention.[3] In subtle and refined ways, patients actively attempt to organize patient-analyst interactions, as we all, hopelessly, engage in the organization of our interpersonal interactions. The analyst seeks the intentional character of these organizational efforts, and listens to hear what a patient wants from him or her as a collaborator in that interaction. However these intentions are formulated and metaphorically described—compulsion, Oedipal complex, penis envy, narcissism, family politics—the patient's attempts to organize the patient-analyst interactions are the only witnessable, experiential "things" available to the analyst, and the only phenomena of interest in the room. These are the "things" which become available for examination and which can be reshaped by reshaping the patient-analyst relationship.

Fundamentally, the terms of diagnosis and the terms that are used to describe the interactions within an analysis—"displacement," "repetition," "regression," "avoidance," "resistance," "transference"—refer to the patterns or "orderlinesses" of patient-analyst interactions which the patient attempts to impose and orchestrate. They are "order terms" used to describe the organizational "work" of the patient; they stand proxy for the phenomena that they describe—the intended orderlinesses of a patient's actions.

In a similar manner, the vocabulary of classical grammar, rhetoric, prosody, and narrative analysis, as well as the new language of open and closed texts, deconstructed subjects, and phallocentric writing, consists of "order terms." They are words which describe natural orderlinesses of the work of reading. They include as well analytic notations such as those of prosodic analysis, for they all refer to and attempt to elucidate prior, self-sufficient organizations of reading's work.

II

Let us compare the use of verbs in the following texts. The first sentence is from Bunyan; it is grammatically incorrect.[4]

When he lift up his foot, he knew not where he should set it next.

The second set of lines are from *The Waste Land*.

And when we were children, staying at the archduke's,
My cousin's, he took me out on a sled,
And I was frightened. He said, Marie,
Marie, hold on tight. And down we went.

In the sentence from Bunyan, the first mistake is that the form of the verb "to lift" does not agree with the subject: the third-person singular in the present tense is "lifts," and in the past tense it is "lifted." The second mistake is that, in this sentence, the verb tenses in the principal and subordinate clauses need to be the same. As a general principle, however, this need not always be so:

> By the time the doctor comes, I shall be dead.

Therein, we begin to see that the problem with the sentence from Bunyan is more involved.

Beneath the description of the errors of Bunyan's sentence, and the dependence of that description on the particular sentence, the idea is that if an event is described as occurring in the past—"when he lifted up his foot"—it needs to stay in the past; if it is described in an indefinite, regular present—"when he lifts up his foot"—it needs to stay in the present. We need not go to a book on grammar to figure this out; the agreement of subject and verb and the consistency of tense between subordinate and principal clauses reflect the way we speak, read, and write. Either of the following emendations will do; the determination of which sentence is the proper one depends on the larger context of reading in which the sentence is embedded.

> When he lifted up his foot, he knew not where he should set it next.

> When he lifts up his foot, he knows not where he should set it next.

In comparison, the lines from *The Waste Land* also involve a change in verb tense. A story from the past is being told, but the verb "to hold" is in the present tense. In contrast to the previous sentence, the change in tense here does not cause a problem. The reader understands that although the events occurred in the past, a speaker in the past would speak of those events as happening "now." The use of verb tense is consistent, and the present tense of the verb "to hold" does not disturb our reading.

Both these situations reflect the ongoing organization of the work of reading; the discovered mistake only makes that work more apparent. The incorrect use of verb tense in Bunyan is found because reading's work has gone awry. "He lift" is wrong and, within context, "he lifted" may make the work of reading right. The tense change involved in "hold on tight" is unremarkable; it is seen but passed over. The unremarkableness of this change in tense is part of a coherent organization of reading that it helps to compose.

In the sentence from Bunyan, the orderlinesses of reading become problematic for the reader. The difficulties are described in terms of a lack of agreement between subject and verb and an inconsistent use of tense. In the lines from Eliot, the verb agrees with the subject and the verb tenses are consistent. The actual phenomena, however, are the preexistent orderlinesses of reading's work and discovered deviations from them. The terms of grammatical analysis are used to describe these orderlinesses. They are "order terms"—descriptions of natural orderlinesses of reading's work that exist prior to and independently of the terms themselves. Bunyan's sentence is not wrong and Eliot's is not right because of the analysis; the analysis articulates what is wrong and right about reading's prior organizational work. "Noun," "verb," "subject," "predicate," "tense," "agreement," "consistency," "subordinate," "principal," and "clause" are parts of a system for describing the work of ordinary reading. As descriptions, they are intended to point to and elucidate the ways in which words are used, not to add anything to reading itself.

III

Like the terms of grammatical analysis, those of rhetoric are also order terms. Consider the "irony" found in Antony's use of "honourable" in his speech at Caesar's burial.[5]

> Friends, Romans, countrymen, lend me your ears;
> I come to bury Caesar, not to praise him.
> The evil that men do lives after them;
> The good is oft interred with their bones.
> So let it be with Caesar. The noble Brutus
> Hath told you Caesar was ambitious.
> If it were so, it was a grievous fault,
> And grievously hath Caesar answer'd it.
> Here, under leave of Brutus and the rest
> (For Brutus is an honourable man;
> So are they all, all honourable men),
> Come I to speak in Caesar's funeral.
> He was my friend, faithful and just to me;
> But Brutus says he was ambitious,
> And Brutus is an honourable man.
> He hath brought many captives home to Rome,
> Whose ransoms did the general coffers fill.
> Did this in Caesar seem ambitious?

> When that the poor have cried, Caesar hath wept;
> Ambition should be made of sterner stuff.
> But Brutus says he was ambitious;
> And Brutus is an honourable man.

No matter how closely the word "honourable" is examined, no irony will be found within it.[6] We do not expect to find irony here, but therein lies the puzzle. What, in actuality, is "irony" being used to describe?

"Irony" refers to the way that we read or hear Antony's speech. There is a hint of irony, for example, in the isolated lines "But Brutus says he was ambitious, / And Brutus is an honourable man." A comparison, signaled by the use of "But," is being made: Brutus is saying something different from what has previously been said; the fact that Brutus is an "honourable man" is offered as justification; if Brutus were dishonorable, the statements he has made might be expected from him. The definiteness of the irony, however, depends on the comparison's being repeated, always as the second part of an insidious contrast: Caesar was a faithful friend, he filled the public coffers, he cried when the poor cried. Antony presents what was known of Caesar and what is now being said about him. The generality of the line "So are they all, all honourable men" also elaborates the "irony": that they all, all of them, are honourable adds doubt to the particular. Antony has been given "leave" to speak, and Antony claims himself as Caesar's friend.

Everything about the speech and its occasion entails the irony surrounding "honourable," and this irony is used to make the point of the speech—the populace should revolt against the dishonorable, ambitious Brutus and his fellow murderers. The word "irony" does not encapsulate the reading of the line; the actual phenomenon of reading or hearing the line is much greater than the word "irony" allows. Moreover, it is not just any "irony," but this particular irony. The this-ness of the phrase, in context, gives pleasure. The use of "irony" draws attention to a prior way of reading or hearing the speech, available before the term is introduced. It speaks of an organization of reading's work—the "context"—from within which the "irony" and the interrelationship of the contextual clues of which it consists are seen. The audience in the pit did not need the apparatus of rhetorical figures to be delighted in the wicked way of Antony's words.

The following lines of Lady Macbeth are also ironic:

> He that's coming
> Must be provided for . . .[7]

Here the word "irony" is used specifically to evoke the context in which the lines are said: Lady Macbeth wishes, on the one hand, to make provisions for the king's visit, but principally to plan the details for his murder. "Irony" supplies part of what is missing from the lines. It restores and reinstitutes a community of readers who find, in reading the line, what is neither in nor not in the line itself.

The uses of "irony" to describe Antony's and Lady Macbeth's lines are, in fact, different. "Honourable" is used by Antony to express its opposite; that is the achievement of his speech. The irony surrounding "provided" involves the ambiguity of the actions to which "provided" refers; Lady Macbeth is speaking about two different things at once. In both cases, the definiteness of the use of "irony" depends on an organization of reading's work; in both, the word "irony" misses the specificity of that particular organization.

The order terms of literary criticism supply an apparatus for describing orderlinesses of reading's work. Descriptions of reading and of reading's achievement—the meaning of a text—clearly are not reading itself. Reading is "more" than its description; it is something real; it is done in detail, in conjunction with a specific text. Like the actions of a patient in analysis, the orderlinesses of reading's work sustain the descriptive cogency of order terms; the term "irony" is justified for Antony's use of "honourable" because "honourable" is embedded in the type of organization of reading that "irony" is used to describe. The prosaic work of reading supports this usage and gives to the use of "irony" the appearance of a self-contained objectivity.

IV

Order terms are intended as part of an analytic system for describing reading's work. As descriptions, however, they are inherently ambiguous. This is apparent in prosodic analysis.

Two texts can have identical scansions and yet have completely different cadence, pace, and patterns of phrasing:[8]

Nót as | a gód, | but as | a gód | might bé,

Ná ked | a mong | them, like | a sa | vage source . . .

What are | the roots | that clutch, | what bran | ches grow

Out of | this sto | ny rub | bish? Son | of man . . .

As with other order terms, scansions attempt to describe a preexistent way of vocalizing lines of poetry. They do not uniquely determine such voicings, nor do they encapsulate the features of the voicings that they attempt to render. They are re-presentations and renderings of voicings, and their authority as descriptions lies within the pretheoretic domain of reading's and hearing's organizational work, not in the renderings themselves. Because of this dependence on reading's work, the same text can be voiced and scanned in different ways:[9]

Áp ril | ís the | crúel lést | mónth,ᴧ | bréed ing

Lí lacs | óut of the | déad lánd, | míx ing

Mém or y | and de síre, | stír ring

Dúll | róots with | spríng ráin.

Ápril is the crúellest mónth, || bréeding

Lílacs out of the déad lánd, || míxing

Mémory and desíre, || stírring

Dúll róots || with spríng ráin.

All these scansions reveal something else as well—a different type of dependence on reading's work. By reading the lines as they are annotated, the reader uses the annotations to find, or to try to find, the actual voicings that the annotated lines represent; in order to find the scansions' cogency as descriptions, a reader must re-embed them within a voicing of the lines. This interrelationship between the voicing of a line and its scansion is also present in the cultivation of a scansion—a text is annotated while being voiced, and the voicing is simultaneously compared with the annotation. In this way, scansions are ambiguous; the descriptions of reading's work that they offer are, at the same time, instructions on how the lines should be read.

This ambiguity of order terms is transparent in scansions and in the multitudinous notational schemes that try to repair that ambiguity. The same ambiguity, however, is present in the use of all order terms.

The following lines illustrate the depth of skill in ordinary reading:

> You blocks, you stones, you worse than senseless things!
> O you hard hearts, you cruel men of Rome!
> Knew you not Pompey?[10]

The reader understands that the repeated "you" indicates that all of the items in the sequence are characterizations of the same people—blocks, stones, senseless things, hard hearts, cruel men. The repetition of "you" gives force to the denunciation; the last item in the list—"you cruel men of Rome"—identifies the list as metaphors for men, and the concluding line tells why they are being described in this way.

The instructional character of this analysis becomes obvious when a reader does not first know how to read the lines. In this case, the analysis provides instructions for reading—that different metaphors are used to describe the same heartless people, those who are celebrating the defeat of Pompey's sons, forgetting the deeds of Pompey for Rome. In a similar manner, the use of the word "irony" directs the reader to find the double meaning in Lady Macbeth's line:

> He that's coming
> Must be provided for . . .

The problematic ambiguity of descriptions as instructions is unavoidable. Descriptions of reading are imprecise, and the gap between a description and actual reading must be filled by reading itself.

The point is made forcefully by the use of the rhetorical term *non sequitur* in the analysis below. The text of *The Waste Land* which the analysis concerns is given first.

> Summer surprised us, coming over the Starnbergersee
> With a shower of rain; we stopped in the colonnade,
> And went on in sunlight, into the Hofgarten,
> And drank coffee, and talked for an hour.

Non sequitur surprises us with "Summer surprised us," imitatively in step. Here subtle scissors begin to cut away connections. Summer surprised us, yes, but with rain, not summeriness. We stopped? "And went on." The conjunction "and" seems absent-minded. Went on, moreover, "in sunlight." A sequence, then, of deadpan surprises. Reversals are simply not indicated as such, apart from the keying word "surprised." One thing at a time. And drank coffee. And talked for an hour. Nothing need, and nothing intends to, follow.[11]

Do these lines need to be read in this way? Could they not be read as incidents of a continuous story: There was a summer shower; people waited in a colonnade, and when the rain stopped, they went into the Hofgarten, had coffee, and talked for a while. By characterizing the lines as consisting of *non sequiturs*, implicit instructions are given for reading the text, and the analysis that follows the characterization elaborates how such a reading might be found. On the one hand, the elaboration tacitly recognizes the insufficiency of the term to describe the work of reading; it attempts to show what, exactly, *"non sequitur"* means in this specific context. On the other hand, simultaneously, the elaboration is designed to teach the cogency of this characterization by showing how *"non sequitur"* can be embedded within the work of reading of the text.

Not only order terms but all characterizations and analyses of a text have this inherent ambiguity as descriptions and instructions. The description of something real is always imprecise; there is always a gap between a description of reading and reading's work. Therein, characterizations and analysis of reading are unavoidably implicit instructions for how a text should be read.

> Women, as Eliot portrays them in *The Waste Land*, are relentlessly self-referenced, whirlpools of vanity, Ophelias on their way down in their own nothingness.
>
> So it is that, in the total context of Marie's monologue, the archduke's instruction, "Marie, / Marie, hold on tight," appears ironic. Marie seems unable to let go of herself, at the same time that she is a deject from her own childhood.[12]

Does Eliot portray all women—and Marie in particular—in this way? Does the archduke speak these lines, and is what he says an "instruction"? Is "hold on tight" ironic? By treating this description of reading as referring to a definite way of reading *The Waste Land*, the reader uses the description as instructions for finding that reading. The definiteness of the description, if it is found, is sustained by an actual reading of the stanza. For other readings of the same text, however, this analysis is clearly inappropriate. The description assumes an already present, definite organization for reading—that the archduke is speaking the lines, that they are ironic, and that Marie has disengaged herself from her childhood experience. It gives implicit instructions to find the organization of reading's work that makes the analysis "true." The description culls a community of readers who can read the stanza in this way; the description is simultaneously, and irreparably, a prescription for how reading's work should be organized.

V

In contrast with singularly occasioned, idiosyncratic descriptions and analyses of texts, order terms have a special property: they belong to systems of descriptive analysis. The order terms of grammar, rhetoric, narratology, and prosody were developed, and continue to be developed, as systems for describing (and, hence, analyzing) the work of reading. As elements of such systems, order terms supply technologies for the competent analysis of reading's work.[13]

At first, the correspondence between an individual order term and the work of reading appears to be direct; each term seems to point to a particular, regularly occurring, extractable orderliness of the work of reading. The irony of Antony's or Lady Macbeth's lines simply points to ways in which the text is read.

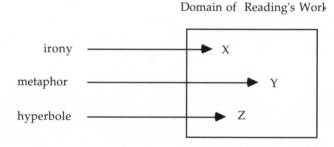

As elements of a descriptive and analytic system, however, the order terms of rhetoric work together; the increasingly fine distinctions that are made between the terms are used to reflect similarly refined distinctions concerning the work of reading. The system is intended to supply technical apparatuses for describing reading's work. The metaphors of Marullus's "You blocks, you stones" are dehumanizing metaphors; they involve hyperbole and anaphora—the repetition of a word or words at the beginning of successive clauses. The lines have a periodic structure—the reader must wait for the question "Knew you not Pompey?" to understand the speaker's intention—and the question itself is rhetorical and ironic; by asking the question, the speaker makes clear the intention and the point of its being asked.[14]

Rather than being depicted in terms of a one-to-one correspondence between the descriptions and specific orderlinesses of reading's work, order terms are better considered in terms of a correspondence between a system of analysis as a whole and its associated domain of phenomena.[15] The order terms of critical analysis constitute competent systems for the descriptive analysis of reading's work.

Rhetorical System   Domain of Reading's Work

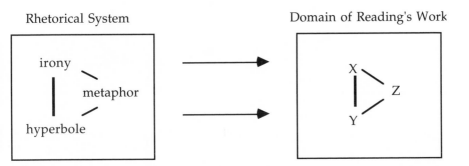

Each such system of order terms generates its own specific domain of analysis; the classical and classically descriptive character of grammar, rhetoric, and prosody is revealed in the fact that their associated domains of phenomena are known by the names of the systems. The idea common to all such systems is that, given any text, the system provides a technical apparatus for competently describing all aspects of reading that text relative to the system's associated domain of phenomena. In the hands of a skilled practitioner, such systems allow fine discriminations in the work of reading a specific text.

Order terms and the intrinsic ambiguity that surrounds their use are part of the technology of reading *cultura*. However, that order terms constitute competent systems of analysis is also relevant to critical reading. The adequacy of such a system to describe the work of reading a particular text is always a local demonstration; it involves the skills of using the system to reveal the work of reading that text. Each individual critical article purports to be such a competent system. Through the analytic framework that it provides, it seeks to reveal a literary demonstration and, therein, the adequacy of that framework to the reading of a text.

As illustrated in the next chapter, the analyses of literary criticism attempt to replicate a systemic structure similar to that of order terms: each critical article attempts to make available a competent system for describing some aspect of reading; each attempts to exhibit the competence of that system to its projected domain of reading's work. Every critical article on a particular text attempts to provide, implicitly through its analysis, a competent system for describing some aspect of the work of reading that text.

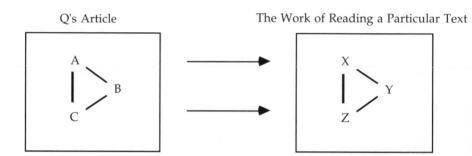

The analytic system itself is not of interest here. The individual systems, and the reasoned discourse, of each professional article are artifacts and residues of the way in which the community of critics reads. The crucial aspect of the relationship between such a competent system and a reading of a text is the way in which this relationship is used. Through this relationship, the ambiguity of characterizations of a text's reading as descriptions and as instructions is embedded within the practices of reading themselves. Through this relationship, critical reading comes to possess its essentially pedagogical or instructed character. And through this relationship, rather than recovering the natural analyzability of reading's work, literary criticism discovers its texts as always deeply reasoned objects.

7.

THE DEEPLY REASONED TEXT

In literary criticism, texts are treated as deeply reasoned objects; each described feature of a text has a reason for its being there. Thus, for one critic, Tiresias is speaking the opening lines of *The Waste Land*, and cloaked allusions in the text help articulate the meaning and organization of his speech.[1] For a different critic, the first stanza of the poem is closely related to ideas developed in *The Golden Bough*: "dull roots" provide a "vegetative analogue to human history and myth," and Marie's journeys to the south are an "unconscious mimicry of the death and disappearance of the god."[2] For another, the opening stanza is imbued with Bradley's philosophy, and Marie's situation is best described in terms of her being "trapped in relational knowledge."[3]

An oddness lies here, for reading is neither logical nor illogical; it is simply the way in which a community reads. The discovered, illogical rationality of the Fortunatus poem is hardly the logic of rational disputation; the poem's irrational rationality is equivalent to the discovery of an unanticipated capability of texts and reading. The stories that Eliot and Thomas tell do not coincide with reasoned discourse; the sniper hides within the lines of Owen's poem; in Juvenal's line, the fact that "genuine tears" make all other tears false is not a matter for deductive logic. Each poetic object is the accomplishment of its text and its reading; the distinctive originality of this accomplishment is what we appreciate. Yet, through critical reading, a text is always found to be a reasoned and reasonable object; its finest details reveal the rational motives for their existence. How does a text come to look like this?

I

In his introductory lectures on physics, Richard Feynman suggests that doing physics is similar to observing a game of chess without being told either the rules or the motives behind any of the moves.[4] Through observation, formulating hypotheses, experimentation, and theorizing, someone might figure out a few of the rules of the game; someone else might determine some of the others. Among a whole group of people, the basic structure of the game might eventually be pieced together.

Let us consider the Fortunatus poem, this time imagining a reader who has little idea of what the poem is about.[5]

> Fortunatus the portrait-painter got twenty sons
> But never one likeness.

Not unlike Feynman's observer, the reader might begin by making some initial observations. "Twenty sons," for example, is hyperbole. It is unlikely that anyone has twenty sons, and there is probably an intrinsic reason for the exaggeration. And why are only sons mentioned? What is the relevance of "sons"—and twenty of them—to the poem? Does Fortunatus's name indicate that he is fortunate, or is the name ironic, and wherein does the irony lie?

Another observation might be that "portrait-painter" is placed in apposition. "Portrait-painter" distinguishes a special property of Fortunatus, but again the relevance of that property is unclear. The fact that a portrait-painter should have sons who look like him or her is not rational argumentation: family resemblance has nothing to do with one's profession. Also, the word "got" is incongruous. The plainest substitute would be "has," but "begat" might do as well. "Got" does not yet have the status of a rhetorical figure, for its intended effect is not understood. If the point of the poem is that Fortunatus's portraits do not resemble their subjects, much as his sons do not resemble him, why is the word "got" employed? It is a distraction.

Each of these descriptions—hyperbole, apposition, incongruous choice of words, irrational argumentation—refers to a pretheoretic, if fragmentary and problematic, organization of the laic skills of reading. To describe "twenty sons" as hyperbole means that a provisional reading has been found that recovers "twenty sons" as an exaggeration, for an effect, however, that is yet unknown.

Such characterizations simultaneously function as minuscule instructions for how the text might be read. As one aspect of the text is described and then another, the associated, underlying work of reading is also being described. Through these characterizations, an increasingly rich texture for reading develops. This texture of reading's work is speculative and promissory, but it is tied to the text and to the arts of reading.

The result is similar to the gestalt animal-in-the-foliage before the animal is found. "Is this the animal? No, it is a branch."[6] The text becomes an "annotated text." Through these annotations, a texture of partial readings of the text is built up.

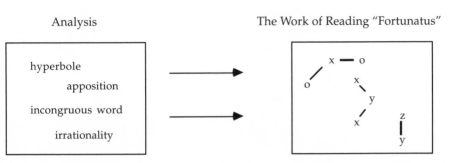

Analysis — The Work of Reading "Fortunatus"

Describing these features of the "text" and manipulating the descriptions also describes and manipulates the work of reading. Reciprocally, such characterizations of the text gain their cogency by articulating how aspects of the text can be read. Against this background of reading that the descriptions cultivate, and against the background of problems that they also engender, the cultured readings of literary criticism are discovered. Descriptions of the text are used to organize and configure a reading that is made available through the organization and configuration of the descriptions.

The Work of Reading "Fortunatus"

```
o — o — o — o
|   |   |   |
x — x — x — x
|   |   |   |
y — y — y — y
```

II

Consider a poetic text as if each letter had been replaced with an "x." Such a figure would represent a text-as-such, the physical object on the page, an imagined text existing before and independently of its reading.

Xxx xxxxx xxxx xxxxxx xxxxxxxxx,
Xxxxxxx xxxx; xxxx xxxxxxxx xxxxxxx
Xxxx xx x xxxxx xxxxxx.

Further, much as we have done before, such a figure could be placed inside a "box." Marginal comments might then be added, each with an arrow from the comment into the "box." Each arrow would point to the place in the text to which the comment refers.

Selected text might also be reinserted in the x'ed-out lines, possibly in bold to highlight their presence and importance.

Treating a text in such a way is not unlike Feynman's game of chess. By observing chess being played, we might notice that the littlest pieces seem to move, most of the time, either one square or two squares straight ahead. When patterns in the reading of a text are observed, features of the text may come to have increased relevance.

Let us return to the examination of the first stanza of *The Waste Land*. A reader might notice, for example, that the verb tenses change from present, to past, and back to present.[7] This is not an "objective" description of the text. The sled ride episode, for example, describes what was said in the past, and therein uses the present tense of the verb "to hold." Similarly, the line in German is read as a line from a conversation in the past, and thus the present tense is explained. The described orderliness of the changing tenses reflects an organization of reading for which the noted changes in tense are the significant changes. Their pattern emerges against a background of pretheoretic reading for which the naturalness of certain verbs is left unquestioned. Circling the relevant verbs— "is," "kept," "read"—the reader might introduce marginal comments, pointing out the pattern of tenses—"present tense," "past tense," "back to present." In this way, such noticings might begin to "surround" a text and come to be embedded in it as "annotations."

Such an annotated text can be cultivated further. In the case of *The Waste Land*, each of the previous descriptions of verb tense seems cogent: the verb "is" in the first line is in the present tense; "kept" is in the past tense. At the same time, the coherence of the scheme of tenses has been lost. It is a puzzle of our own devising. In the earlier reading of this stanza, the changing tenses reflected the recollections of a woman remembering events of her past. Now, no longer tied to a prior poetic object, the present description raises the question of why the tenses change. The remarkable changes in tense—from present to past to present—become a feature of the text which needs attention. At once, the reading of the text has been made mysterious, and yet a small eddy of structure for reading has been generated—the orderly progression of verb tense. It is a structure that subsequently can be enriched.

As a conjecture, let us suppose that the entire text of *The Waste Land* is spoken by one person. Although this is not unreasonable for the first stanza, such an assumption causes problems for reading *The Waste Land* as a whole. A woman seems to be speaking in one place, a man in another, a prophet in another, a somewhat and temporarily disengaged narrative voice in another. If one person is speaking all these lines, the picture of a hermaphroditic ventriloquist's puppet suffering from a multiple personality disorder is not entirely inappropriate. The serious point is that a problem of pronouns arises.

In the earlier reading, the pronouns fit together as a coherent scheme of reference. "Us" was all of us; "we" was Marie and her lover; "he" was her lover; "you" was Marie's way of referring to herself; and "I" was Marie. If a single person is speaking throughout the entire poem, it certainly is not Marie. But in this case, who is this speaker? Who are the "us" of winter, the "we" of the Hofgarten, the woman who speaks in German, and how did Marie get mixed up in all this? Clearly, there are a number of different pronouns within the opening stanza. The pronouns cease to provide a coherent scheme of reference. Is there an underlying scheme, or is the lack of one intentional?

In addition to the scheme of pronouns, a difference between the events of summer and the line in German can be noted. The events of summer describe a "visual" memory, whereas the line in German is an auditory one. The characterization seems cogent, but there is no compelling reason for giving it priority. The description elucidates a contrast—a difference in reading—between the lines. This contrast might also be articulated as the difference between a fixation with particulars—this shower, this cup of coffee—and an abstract proposition concerning national identity. Both descriptions shade the reading of the text that they are intended to characterize.

In this same stanza, there is also progression backward in time from April to winter to summer. Why has Eliot left out autumn—or, to put it in another way, why is there just this triad of seasons? The question seems irrelevant to the earlier reading; now that it is raised, is there a reason for it? Is there a repetitive pattern of "threes" throughout *The Waste Land* that is integrally tied to the way we should organize our reading of the text?

Finally, the title of the first section of *The Waste Land* seems to have removed the first three words of the name of the burial service in the Church of England—"The Order for the Burial of the Dead." The "theme" of this service might be summarized as "resurrection." Certainly, this has a bearing on the opening stanza of *The Waste Land* where April, the time of rebirth, is viewed with displeasure. Moreover, Eliot's opening lines provide a marked contrast to the opening lines of Chaucer's *The Canterbury Tales,* where the rains of April are praised. Eliot's lines mix up the elements of Chaucer's description, putting them to a different purpose. The Marie of *The Waste Land* might also be associated with a real person, a countess named Marie Larisch; there are some parallels, not the least of which is the name, and Eliot may have actually met her or read her autobiography. Eliot may be using these sources purposefully and relying on the reader to know them and to understand their intended relevance. What are Eliot's motives for doing so? How is the relevance of these possible references recovered through a reading of the poem?

All these noticings could be added as commentary in the margins of *The Waste Land.* The conjectured consistent voice of a single protagonist could be written at the top of the page; the references to Chaucer's *Canterbury Tales,* the burial service of the Church of England, and Marie Larisch might appear with arrows pointing to the relevant lines. Groups of lines might be circled in the text and marked as a seasonal progression from April to winter to summer. Lines might be contrasted for their visual or auditory character. Selected pronouns—"us," "we," "I," "you"—might be underlined and joined together with lines. The image is of a text crowded with commentary, immersed in and entangled with a reader's descriptions of it.

Alternative descriptions of the opening stanza of *The Waste Land* are certainly possible: a number of different voices may be speaking the lines; the changing seasons may reflect mythic cycles of nature, etc. Independently of these other possibilities, each of the given descriptions does "annotate" the text, and each "annotation," in and of itself, cogently describes some aspect of the laic skills of reading that text: the change in verb tense, the problematic scheme of pronominal references, a borrowing from the life of a real person, the possible continuity of a single speaker of the lines, the cloaked allusions to Chaucer and the burial service of the Church of England. Superimposed on a text, such annotations reflect initial attempts at organizing the work of reading. At the same time, they provide a preliminary filter through which a text is read. They embed a text in a fragmented texture of the reading's work. They also problematize that work and the laic skills of which it consists: What is the reason for the triad of seasons? What schemes of reference explain the pronouns and the changes in the tense of the verbs? What purpose does the allusion to Chaucer serve? By problematizing reading, the annotations simultaneously justify the need for their introduction. The annotated text reflects the missing continuity and coherence of reading that the annotations seek to address.

Through such annotations, the critic builds an increasingly dense texture for reading's work. To put together the tangram in Figure 9 as a square, the puzzle solver arranges and rearranges the parts to find how they might compose such an object. By shifting, modifying, and arranging textual annotations, the critic organizes and rearranges the laic skills of reading. The "animal" emerges from the foliage; an organizational gestalt of reading emerges from this increasingly rich texture of reading's work. The shift in verb tense is intended to distract the reader from looking for a story; the pronouns refer to an abstract schema where, for example, "you" refers to Eliot's personal "me"; the triad of seasons is but one of a multiplicity of triads used to articulate the metaphysical meaning of the poem.[8] This discovered organization of reading is tied to the way in which the annotations—the descriptions of the text—are fitted together. In that each piece is a reasoned object, in that the annotations are manipulated together in reasonable and accountable ways, the discovered reading and its text are discovered as already, and hopelessly, deeply reasoned objects.

Figure 9

III

The preceding section contains an element of caricature; to remove it, we must re-embed the annotated text in the arts of reading as practiced by the critical community. The annotated text is a reflection of those practices, arising as part of a gestalt of reading rather than as a matter of explicit construction. It is part of an "instructed reading." An instructed reading is a discovered, demonstrable, accountable "reading"; within it, the arts of reading and their associated, annotated text are intrinsically and naturally connected, arising and developing together as deeply reasoned objects.

Let us consider the following excerpts from an analysis by Calvin Bedient of the opening stanza of *The Waste Land*.

> Under the aegis of [paradox], the lovely *incipit* of Chaucer's *Canterbury Tales* (virtually the *incipit* of English poetry) is turned on its head in "April is the cruellest month." To rhyme "April" with "cruel"! . . . Even English prosody is queered as the first three lines fall a syllable short of iambic pentameter. . . . Deceptive Chaucerian beauty of measure is flouted, no line is an "expected" English line. . . .[9]

> "Summer," by contrast, is unequivocally a certain summer, implicitly datable, and dated, and the Starnbergersee stands in its own geographical space. So with the colonnade, the hour, the talk. Significations here are single-leveled. Firm. Trustworthy. The "world" of the first seven lines is patently a fictional construct, a molecular model of a certain state of feeling. . . .[10]

> *Non sequitur* surprises us with "Summer surprised us," imitatively in step. Here subtle scissors begin to cut away connections. Summer surprised us, yes, but with rain, not summeriness. We stopped? "And went on." The conjunction "and" seems absent-minded. Went on, moreover, "in sunlight." A sequence, then, of deadpan surprises. Reversals are simply not indicated as such, apart from the keying word "surprised." One thing at a time. And drank coffee. And talked for an hour. Nothing need, and nothing intends to, follow.[11]

> Meanwhile, Marie's speech is broken indeed. Not only does it begin abruptly (if with a pseudo-smoothing connective); once it gets started, it darts, and darts again, like a minnow that has lost its school. *Non sequitur* governs her monologue, just as it does the three- (or four-) discourse structure of the paragraph.[12]

> . . . there are Lithuanians who consider "echt deutsch"anything but Lithuanian. Political temporization? In any case, Marie, all temporization, does not follow from the German with her "And," nor her talk of the fright of sledding that leads, abruptly, to "In the mountains, there you feel free." Marie examines nothing; she only declares, and serially. . . . She rejects the chains of perceived connections: not

"But now I only read,"; instead, "I read." Even the rhythm of the last line disavows any relation to the previous one: the excited jounce of "In the mountains, there you feel free" gives way to the nervous twinge of interruption in the bored, dismissive rhythms of "I read, much of the night, and go south in the winter."[13]

These quotations appear contentious in all their aspects. The opening three lines of the stanza seem poorly described as "a syllable short of iambic pentameter." In that the opening lines of the Prologue of *The Canterbury Tales*, with their regular rhythms, are sometimes glossed as iambic pentameter, Bedient's description appears to be a device by which to attach the earlier poem to Eliot's lines. Is Eliot purposefully manipulating English measure? Does *non sequitur* really characterize the description of the events of that summer day, or are those events simply part of a continuous story in which a couple runs for shelter and ends up having coffee and talking? What are the grounds for reading the line in German as part of a conversation, seemingly overheard and distracting the protagonist,[14] and does this not imply an unexplicated continuity in the lines? Is Marie's speech broken, and does she babble on like a child rushing to tell a story?[15] Does the line "In the mountains, there you feel free" reflect the hurried excitement of the sled ride or a distancing of Marie from it?

Bedient frames his descriptions by what Eliot does not say: the connective "and" is a "pseudo-smoothing connective"; the rhythms of the opening lines are heard to lack a syllable that would make them iambic pentameter; Marie, if she were reflective, would say, "But now I only read." Bedient points to what the text lacks to explain why it lacks what he claims is lacking: continuity, rhythmic articulation, reflective perception. He describes an annotated text, marked by partial scansions, a convoluted reference to another text, discontinuities, paradox, *non sequitur*, overheard utterances, an unreflective voice that babbles on.

The heart of Bedient's reading of this stanza is described in the following lines:

> Who speaks the first seven lines? How persuasive are we meant to find them? And who speaks the next four, and the line in German? And who is the final speaker, this Marie who begins talking as if she needed no introduction?
>
> No poem before ever started so, with an "overhear me," then an "overhear *me*," and the same again, and all the while a "never mind who, for it scarcely matters anyway."
>
> It *is* going to matter who, and quite soon, but first the poem registers a crisis of heteroglossia, and, beyond that, a crisis of meaningless identity.[16]

First, Bedient is telling us to read the text as being divided into four sections. It might be just as cogent to divide the text into seven sections—one for each season, the line in German, the sled episode, and each of the two last lines—but let us do as Bedient suggests. The poem begins with a somber voice, reflecting a certain life, commenting on things bound up with spring; a second voice tells of events in the Hofgarten (coffee and conversation); a third voice, speaking in German, takes pride in her claimed nationality; and the stanza concludes with the voice of Marie, recounting a sled ride and, therein, revealing something of her present life.

When the text is read in this manner, the differences between these "sections" become heightened. The first set of lines are short and morose, and express feelings about the human condition; the summer vignette is light-hearted and describes particular events; the line in German makes a personal statement in German, it concerns an abstraction, it is a literal quotation of some indeterminate person; Marie relates a personal, frightening incident from her childhood.

Bedient, however, tells us more. Rather than disjointed utterances, Bedient claims the voices are competing with each other to be overheard. The voice of April is interrupted by the voice of summer, as the line in German and Marie's speech interrupt the voices preceding them. Each of the voices is part of a larger text that is muted by the voice which now gains prominence. Rather than a medley of speakers, we have new voices which drown out the preceding ones.

The image that Bedient gives is that of the beginning of a play: each of the actors is already on a darkened stage; each is speaking, but inaudibly; the spotlight shifts as each, in turn, speaks louder, claiming a right to be "overheard." Each of the actors announces something about himself or herself indirectly, through his or her lines, and therein something about the play as a whole. The first voice begins:

> April is the cruellest month, breeding
> Lilacs out of the dead land, mixing

A second voice intrudes, drowning out the first, as if the first voice kept on talking but we are no longer able to hear it:

> Summer surprised us, coming over the Starnbergersee
> With a shower of rain; we stopped in the colonnade,

A third voice is now clumped on top of the other two—a single line of an overheard conversation, drifting across the tables, obtruding on the second voice and attracting our (or a protagonist's) attention:

Bin gar keine Russin, stamm' aus Litauen, echt deutsch.

Finally, the voice of Marie is overheard above the others, caught *in media res* as if she were already speaking, requiring attention because she wants to talk, not because of what she has to say.

> And when we were children, staying at the archduke's,
> My cousin's, he took me out on a sled,

A more textual image of the way that Bedient reads is also possible. Each of the "voices" would have its own script, written on rectangles of paper and containing lines much greater that those that appear in *The Waste Land*. The pieces of paper would be positioned on top of one another, blocking out the rest of the preceding voice's speech.

By organizing the skills of reading to give cogency to Bedient's description of them, Bedient is seen as describing an actual, realizable way of reading the text. The individual voices present a pastiche of speech, glued together as if in a collage. One voice interrupts another, not with the intention of being heard—that is, not directed specifically toward the reader—but simply to get its chance to be overheard. The gloominess of the first lines contrasts with the second speaker, someone seemingly lost in the particularities of particular events. For this speaker, there is no connection between the events, just this coffee and just this conversation. The fourth voice, Marie, does begin in the middle of some story; she rushes to tell the story, revealing, but unable to reflect on, its deeper significance.

> So it is that, in the total context of Marie's monologue, the archduke's instruction, "Marie, / Marie, hold on tight," appears ironic. Marie seems unable to let go of herself, at the same time that she is a deject from her own childhood. Marie cannot say from what she feels excluded, but the childlikeness of her discourse—the breathless polysyndeton of the first lines, the flitbrained parataxis of the final ones—reveals what it is, namely the excited openness of childhood.[17]

Thus, the opening stanza "registers a crisis of heteroglossia, and, beyond that, a crisis of meaningless identity." The other quotations from Bedient's commentary make sense as a descriptive analysis of a reading of the text; the reader understands the annotated text in and as a reading of the text itself. We notice as well the fine detail of Bedient's reading, the instructional nature of its characterizations, and the deeply reasoned character of the revealed text.

Once Bedient's reading of the opening stanza is found, his commentary is recovered as a cogent, descriptive analysis of that reading. Equally, the initially fragmentary and problematic readings that underlie his commentary, like the tiles of a tangram, now provide a coherent reading of the stanza. Rather than a tangram in pieces, the pieces fit together as a square (Figure 10). The unified figure is the "instructed reading," something visible and concrete, an actual reading of the text. Yet, at the same time, this achievement is seen in terms of the fitting together of the pieces; it is a revelation not only through but of the pieces which compose it. Eliot's text, as it appears on the page, does not necessarily—naturally—read this way.

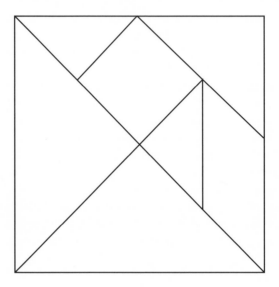

Figure 10

Nowhere in Bedient's writings is an annotated text actually present. Instead, the text of Bedient's analysis is cut away in certain places to exhibit beneath it the original text-as-such that he analyzes. The exegetical text surrounds the explicated text; we read Eliot's text through the windows which the analysis provides. All our efforts at reading appear to be directed toward this underlying text, toward revealing the descriptiveness of the original text for its own reading.

An ambiguous shifting between perspectives is involved: the framing devices of the analysis are used to exhibit a reading of the original text, yet readers implicitly are asked to read that prior text as an explication of the framework. The original text stands proxy for the annotated text, and the analysis that surrounds the original text offers itself as the achievement of our work of reading. The text is read in order to make the analysis true, and the annotated text is the achievement of this reading. The annotations become inscribed in the reading itself.

IV

Instructed readings have two interrelated problems. These problems "live" within critical reading and are recognized by its practitioners: First, instructed readings involve a "distortion" of the laic arts of reading; they add "something" to, or modify, the skills of reading *simpliciter*. Second, their instructional character comes to be embedded within the reading of the text; the instructed reading itself is an achievement. A reader can organize the skills of reading to find the different voices that Bedient describes, to see how Marie begins, breathlessly, *in media res*. But the reader must willfully shape the laic skills of reading in order to do so; the reader must remember how the text should be read in order to find Bedient's reading. Bedient's reading hopelessly retains its instructed character in order for the reader to read the text in the manner that he describes.

Bedient gives reasons for everything—for what the text says and for what it does not say; why the first seven lines consist of "paradoxes" and the later ones of *"non sequiturs"*; why there are different voices, why they overlap, and why Marie babbles on. Eliot's text has become, and is seen as, a deeply reasoned and reasonable object. The instructed reading arises from within and necessitates such reasoning. Why else would one read the text in this way? The reasoning is not the simplistic reasoning of dialectic argumentation. That Marie babbles is tied to the fact that she begins speaking in line 13; that she begins speaking in line 13 is tied to the presence of other speakers trying to be "overheard"; that she speaks in a certain way is available through the contrast with the other voices. The instructed reading offers itself as a gestalt of reasoning for the text to be read in that way. The text is discovered as a deeply reasoned object.

8.

THE INSTRUCTED READING

The poetic object reshapes and molds the work of reading to its text. It is an original articulation of the laic skills of reading, discovered through, in, and as its naturally analyzable text, created and found as a text embedded in the ordinary skills of reading. It is an object that belongs to the craft of poetic composition.

The instructed reading is the critics' object. It is an achievement of the arts of critical reading and reveals a deeply reasoned text, one whose details reflect the motives for their presence. As an object, an instructed reading is greater than its exegetical analysis and different from it. An instructed reading provides a version, or a reflected image, of a poetic object. It provides a version of the work of reading as well.

Like the poetic object, an instructed reading depends on and shapes the laic skills of reading, but it distorts those laic skills at the same time. In order for this distortion of ordinary reading to be found, the natural analyzability of reading's work must be examined in greater detail.

I

The following story and questions recall material that might be found in a test of reading comprehension for children in late primary school.[1]

> Amy is an automobile mechanic. She lives with Dad and me. Last week, we invited my friend Hannah, and all of us went to look at new cars. Amy opened the hoods and showed us the engines. We did not understand everything that Amy said, but it was fun to hear her talk. Next, Dad test drove two cars and we got to ride in the back seat. The very best was the convertible. It was red with black leather upholstery. It had a V8 engine, a four-barrel carburetor, and could go from 0 to 60 miles per hour in about four seconds. After looking at the cars, Amy took us out for pizza; it was Amy's turn to cook dinner.

1. Who wrote this story?
   a) Hannah
   b) Amy
   c) Dad
   d) Hannah's friend

2. Which reason is *not* given for the children liking the convertible?
   a) the miles per gallon
   b) the color of the car
   c) the speed of the car
   d) the type of motor

3. Where did the children get their knowledge about the convertible?
   a) From what Amy said and showed them
   b) From their friends at school
   c) From a television commercial
   d) From Amy performing mechanical tests

4. In the seventh sentence, what does the phrase "the very best" refer to?
   a) Story
   b) Test drive
   c) Convertible
   d) Car

5. What reason does the writer of the story *suggest* for going out for pizza?
   a) Pizza tastes good.
   b) Everybody was hungry.
   c) Amy does not like to cook.
   d) Nobody likes Amy's cooking.

How is the right answer to the first question found? The story is written as first-person narration: the narrator refers to himself or herself as a "me," to Hannah as "my friend," and to various groups of people as "we" and "us." The person who wrote the story is an "I." This does not answer the question, but it is consequential: if there is a "writer" of the story, reading the text must reveal a coherence of the pronominal references. In fact, this coherence is the real question behind the question of who "wrote" the story. The actual author is inconsequential; the question is who is indicated as the writer through the reading of the story.

The "writer" of the story is evidently not Amy because Amy lives with "Dad and me"; it is not Dad because "Dad" refers to the father of the person telling the story; it is not Hannah because Hannah is "my friend." These are not correct answers. Yet, reading the story does not make plain that "Hannah's friend" is the writer either. "Hannah's friend" is one possible description of the writer, inferred from the fact that Hannah is the friend of the writer and that the relation of friendship, in this context, can be symmetrical: if Hannah is "my" friend, "I" am Hannah's friend. The appropriateness of the answer, rather than the answer itself, reflects the analyzability of our work of reading the text. Through the text, the reader inspects the practices of reading to find the rationality of those practices that the question and possible answers help to articulate.

A similar situation occurs for the other questions. The subtleties of Question 2, however, lie in the question, not in the search for the right answer. First, the question refers to "children." That some of the people in the story are "children" is not explicit, but a cogent and appropriate inference given our practices of reading and speaking. The story is written in a way that a child might write; it tells things that a child might say; it refers to a friend and "me" who were taken along by Amy and Dad to look at cars. Second, nothing in the story says explicitly that the children "liked" the convertible; the convertible is offered only as "the very best." On the surface, this is an assertion of fact. The question and the possible answers articulate the natural analyzability of the passage: the use of "best" signals an opinion; the particular enumerated features of the convertible, in their particularity and in the manner of their expression, are read as supporting the identification of an assertion of fact— the best—with a preference—liking one car over the others.

The practical import of Question 2 is different from the intricacies of the question. The question asks the reader to compare the list of answers to the features of the car given in the story; the question requires that the reader see through the technical details to the practical task that is involved and to answer appropriately, therein finding what is really being asked. Question 2 depends essentially on the negative form in which it is phrased. It does not seek to identify a definite state of affairs—what virtues make the convertible "the very best." Instead, it clarifies how reading is done and the natural analyzability of doing it by clarifying that which cannot be said about its accomplishment, that which reading the passage cannot be twisted to say.

For the third question, the most likely inference is that the children got their knowledge about the convertible from what Amy told them and showed them about the car. The story does not introduce their friends from school, nor does it refer to a television commercial the children might have seen. It does not mention Amy testing the convertible; if she had, this might have been a prominent feature of the narration. Instead, Amy lifted up the hoods of various cars, showed the children the engines, and talked about the cars. The car that the children liked the best was the convertible. The details concerning the convertible are seen, given the choice of answers, to be what Amy must have said. Did

Amy tell them about the convertible? The mute text-in-itself does not say this; instead, the proper answer reflects a discovered orderliness of reading's work. The relevance of the question and the adequacy of the answer arise not because they are the objective thing that the text says but because the analyzability embedded in reading provides for that relevance and adequacy.

Question 4 is closest to the natural analyzability of reading. "The very best," in fact, ultimately refers to the convertible, but the question asks the reader to see the readably inherent logic of the construction. The convertible is selected as one of a collection, and the collection is that of the cars the children got to see: the convertible is "the very best" of the cars. This reasoning reflects the analyzability already embedded in the activity of reading as its ongoing accomplishment and self-sustaining grounds. Yet, at the same time, the explicit articulation of that reasoning is generated by the question.

The last question, Question 5, appears to go beyond a reading of the text. The writer of the story only "suggests" a reason for going out for pizza; the question, with its selection of answers, seems to indicate a context of uncertainty. Consider, however, the sentence to which the question refers: "After looking at the cars, Amy took us out for pizza; it was Amy's turn to cook dinner." The first principal clause describes an event—"Amy took us out for pizza"; the second gives an explanation of why she did this—"it was Amy's turn to cook dinner." Given this way of reading, neither of the first two answers could be correct, not because they do not refer to real circumstances—that many people like pizza and that people try to eat when they are hungry—but because these answers miss the causality that is established through the arts of reading. Choosing between the remaining answers depends on seeing that it is Amy's preference to go out for pizza "because" it is her turn to cook; nothing is said about the others not liking Amy's cooking. The subtlety of the sentence, and the question, is that this preference resides in the juxtaposition of the clauses, how we read that juxtaposition, and that we see the preference being expressed through that juxtaposition, therein as the purposeful construction of its author. We read the sentence not as saying what Amy said; its construction suggests how the author interpreted Amy's actions.

What does such a test tell us about reading? At first, the test seems to ask a child to read the story and then answer the questions in terms of the content of what the child has read: What color was the convertible's upholstery? Black. What did the children have for dinner? Pizza. Reading and reading comprehension, if related, are treated as somewhat distinct. The questions above, however, indicate a different intention: they attempt to reveal how the child is involved in the activity of reading itself.

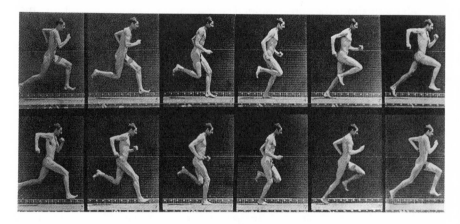

Figure 11

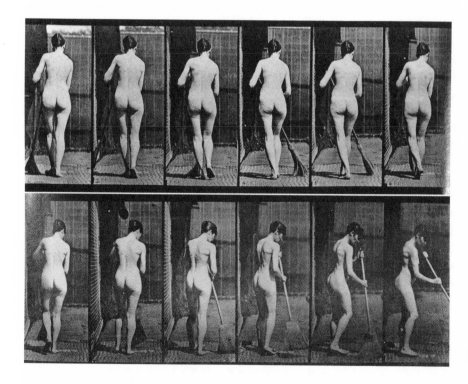

Figure 12

All of the questions seek to determine whether a child is engaged in the prior, naturally analyzable work of reading. "Natural analyzability" does not refer to explicit analyses of that work. The questions, their reasonableness, and the reasonableness of the answers clarify the intrinsic reasoning and rationality already possessed by reading's lived work. The extent to which a reader is engaged in that work is what, in fact, such tests seek to assess.

II

When the two sequences of photographs in Figures 11 and 12 are viewed, we do not see a man running and a woman sweeping with a broom.[2] We see depictions of these actions. We are witnesses to them as depictions, as accounts of a "running man" and a "woman sweeping with a broom." The photographs are frozen moments of continuous actions which, as a sequence of photographs, exhibit their character as representations of running and sweeping. The distinction between seeing a running man and seeing a depiction of a running man is consequential; it points to the work that we have to do to see the depiction. Because of this work, the sequences retain their representational character.

What the sequences of photographs depict is not solely a property of the photographs or their arrangement. As we look at the photographs, we engage in a small bit of analysis. We examine the pictures in a sequence to make sure that they are all of the same person. We follow the feet and legs of the runner, from left to right in the pictures on the page, observing that the left leg is coming to be placed on the ground, that it meets the ground, and that the right leg is being propelled in front of it. The stretch of the legs and the movement of the arms reflect running, not walking. Each position is analyzably a sequentially next position of a runner while running, and therein we see the sequence as reflecting that action. The pictures of the sweeper are examined as a similar sequence of movements. The viewer finds the sweeping motion of the broom from the sweeper's left to her right, and scrutinizes the way the bristles of the broom are bent. The left-to-right ordering of the photographs is recovered as the sequential character of the woman's movements. The woman, analyzably, turns to her right and sweeps again toward her right and out toward the camera. Her head follows the motion of the broom as the action of a sweeper attending to his or her work. In the final four stills, she plants her left leg as she pushes to her right.

Through such minute but unremarkable and ordinary analyses, the viewer recovers the left-to-right sequencing of the photographs as a reflection of the temporal organization of the actions that the sequences depict. Whatever else the pictures show, they exhibit stages of continuous actions—running and sweeping. The propriety of our analyses lies in what the pictures, through those analyses, observably exhibit—depictions of someone running and of someone sweeping with a broom. The explication of such an analysis is not the natural analyzability of the photographs; the term refers to a prior "seeing" of the sequences that has that analyzability embedded in it.

The natural analyzability of seeing required by the Muybridge photographs is similar to the natural analyzability of reading that underlies tests of reading comprehension. The following modified cloze passage shows this similarity:

> One night Bobo was playing with the dog. "Roll over," he said. But the __1__ would not __2__ over. It ran across the floor after a ball. Then round and __3__ it went with the __4__ in its mouth. Bobo __5__ not far behind.[3]

Consider the missing words 1 and 2. In the sentence preceding these deletions, "Roll over" is an imperative; Bobo ("he") is commanding the dog to roll over. The use of "But" in the third sentence offers a contrast between the intention of the command—that the dog should "roll over"—and the response of the dog. The connection, however, is more complex: the contrast is stressed with the use of "would not"; the partially deleted phrase "____ over" repeats the structure of the "Roll over" in the previous sentence; the only "the" around is "the dog."

Realizing that the third sentence should read "But the dog would not roll over" is similar to finding the depiction of the running man or the woman sweeping with the broom. The depiction of continuous action in the photographs does not depend on an explicit analysis. If all our actions and reasoning had to be made explicit, the world would make us crazy. Yet, as practice, something like that analysis must be done in order for the sequences of pictures to be seen for what they are—ordered sequences of pictures. Similarly, the analyzability of the cloze passage does not depend on the ability to articulate it. Children at an appropriate level of reading skill can fill in the blanks.

For the cloze passage, the achievement—finding the appropriate words— is tied to the observable propriety of those words as the appropriate words. This, in turn, is no different from the analyzability of the passage: the dog is that which would not roll over but, instead, went round and round with Bobo not far behind. The missing words force the reader to attend to the intrinsic rationality of the work of reading the passage, articulated not in an analysis of that natural analyzability but in finding the words that exhibit it.

Studies of reading comprehension examine the natural analyzability of reading; they treat the competent reader as a person for whom that natural analyzability is available. Literary criticism also takes the analyzability of reading as its phenomenon, but does so through "instructed readings." An instructed reading attempts to exhibit the analyzability of reading; in doing so, however, it turns the natural analyzability of reading into something different—an "objective," justifiable way of reading a text.[4] This objectively accountable way of reading recovers a text's details as evidence for its way of reading, and it is seen as a substitute, and as a corrective, for the laic skills of reading *simpliciter*.

III

The captioned photographs that are found in introductory sociology textbooks illuminate the type of transformation of reading *simpliciter* involved in instructed readings, as well as reveal the familiarity of such transformations.[5]

Consider two such photographs.[6] The first is a picture of a city street in which a man lies face up near the curb and two bicyclists are passing by. The rear bicyclist is looking forward, possibly at the man in the street; the bicyclist nearest the man has her head turned away from the body, one hand raised to the side of her face. Whether she is looking at something and pulling back her hair, avoiding having her picture taken, or specifically not looking at the man lying in the street is unclear. The man in the street may be a drunk; he has probably not been shot and is probably not dead. It is a city scene: cars are on the street; buildings are multilevel; people in the background are engaged in different activities.

In the second photograph, a person, possibly a woman, is in a stationary pose indicative of "waiting": arms straight at her sides, her right leg straight, her left foot bent at the ankle.[7] She is wearing a tank top with gold trim, hot pants, and high-heeled sandals. Her back is turned to the camera and her face cannot be seen. It is night; street and car lights are on; a man, dressed somewhat shabbily, is walking down the sidewalk. Bags of trash and a trash bin are on the sidewalk.

Disengaged from the context in which they were taken, the pictures lack any obvious thematic content, except the sheer presence of the scenes—a man, apparently unconscious, lying face up in a wide business street; a glimpse of night life in the inner city. In contrast to these unthematic observations,[8] the captions associated with the photographs offer the scenes as illustrations of specific social phenomena. For the first picture, urbanites are said to selectively respond to features in their environment and, in particular, to "tune out" the poor and homeless:

> As Simmel points out, urbanites tend to respond selectively to their environment. For many Americans, tuning out the poor and homeless is a response to feeling powerless to help.[9]

Is the man lying in the street homeless or poor? Even if one of the bicyclists is "tuning out," is the other? If they are selectively responding to their environment, are they doing this because of their feelings of powerlessness? Are the cyclists "urbanites" or visitors to the city? Did Simmel point this out, and if he did, is this photograph what he meant?

In the second photograph, the central figure may be a prostitute, but the definiteness of this statement is not apparent, nor is the fact that this person is not paying his or her taxes. The caption, however, reads:

> Illegal activities such as prostitution are part of the underground economy, whose income goes unreported and untaxed.[10]

The descriptions that the captions offer are plausible, but not transparent from the photographs.

Rather than trying to state and analyze the obvious, the captions beneath the photographs describe social phenomena for which the photographs could provide potential illustrations. The bicyclist is "tuning out the poor and homeless" because of her feelings of powerlessness to help. The "prostitute" is a symbol of an underground economy; the income derived from prostitution is unreported and untaxed; prostitutes are tax-evaders. The authority for the captions does not lie within the natural analyzability of the photographs, nor is that natural analyzability interrogated. Instead, the captions shift attention away from the photographs to the adequacy of the photographs as indicators of, and as evidence for, general structures of social action. The student who questions whether, in fact, the bicyclist is "tuning out" or whether the person is a prostitute or does not pay taxes has missed the purpose of the illustrations.

Once the phenomenon—the gap between photograph and caption—is seen, it becomes available throughout introductory textbooks.[11] A photograph of a drunk slumped against a building with a bottle raised is given the following caption:

Some people come to view themselves wholly in terms of their deviant status, for example, as nothing but a drunk.[12]

A shot of children climbing a wall is captioned:

There is often a very serious side to play. For instance, King of the Mountain imparts important lessons about success and power.[13]

For a photograph of three elderly people sitting on a bench, the two women facing each other and talking, the man at the side apparently attending to the conversation, the caption says:

A distinctive characteristic of a triad is that the social bond between two of the members can exclude the third.[14]

Beneath a picture of an elderly Japanese man and woman seated some distance apart and facing away from each other, the caption reads:

Sociologists who conduct research in other countries should be aware that what they may think are "innocent questions" may cause discomfort or even offense to others. In many societies, people rarely discuss their sexual habits with strangers or even with each other. Thus some of the questions asked by Blumstein and Schwartz would probably offend the typical Japanese couple. The growing social diversity of the United States raises the importance of this kind of sensitivity for research carried out at home as well.[15]

Are the people in this photograph a "typical Japanese couple" or a couple at all? Have they been asked a question about their sexual habits? Would they be offended if they had, and does the photograph reveal discomfort?

In their serious use, captioned photographs are part of a pedagogy for teaching students to see the social world in terms of sociological analysis. That analysis is different from the appearances of the social world. In sociology, students must be trained to view the familiar, ordinary world of everyday action as providing indicators of the structures of action that lie beneath it. The captions use the natural analyzability of action—the possible ways in which the photographs could be seen—and distort and transform it, making the photographs into evidence for interpretations of them. Their authority comes to lie within the objectivity of the social phenomena that the photographs are intended to illustrate, and in our ability to see the photographs as possible illustrations of those phenomena.

IV

Let us return to Calvin Bedient's analysis of a passage from *The Waste Land*. The relevant lines of the *The Waste Land* are repeated first.

> Summer surprised us, coming over the Starnbergersee
> With a shower of rain; we stopped in the colonnade,
> And went on in sunlight, into the Hofgarten,
> And drank coffee, and talked for an hour.

> *Non sequitur* surprises us with "Summer surprised us," imitatively in step. Here subtle scissors begin to cut away connections. Summer surprised us, yes, but with rain, not summeriness. We stopped? "And went on." The conjunction "and" seems absent-minded. Went on, moreover, "in sunlight." A sequence, then, of deadpan surprises. Reversals are simply not indicated as such, apart from the keying word "surprised." One thing at a time. And drank coffee. And talked for an hour. Nothing need, and nothing intends to, follow.[16]

The first oddity of this reading is the definiteness it gives to the word "surprised." If April is "the cruellest month" and winter "kept us warm," then the surprise of summer might well be that there was a summer. In other words, "Summer surprised us." In this case, the poetic construction is that summer "personified" is itself "coming over the Starnbergersee / With a shower of rain."

Bedient, in contrast, points to the rain as that which caused surprise. People were walking; they were caught in a sudden shower. Since this could be described as a "surprise," Bedient slightly twists the construction "Summer surprised us" to "summer surprised us because of the rain." The surprise of summer does resonate with the "surprise" of being caught in a summer shower, but the laic skills of reading have been gently skewed in order to get the lines to say this. Bedient's claim may well be that the connection he has supplied is intended by Eliot, who purposely made that connection oblique in order to lead the reader to this reading.

A similar skewing is found in Bedient's reading of the other events of summer. The description in the poem may no more consist of *non sequiturs* than any account of a day's events: people were caught in a shower of rain; they waited in a colonnade; when the rain broke, in the sunlight, they went into the Hofgarten, had a cup of coffee, and talked together. Bedient invites us to divorce the text from the continuity of the events that the laic skills of reading supply. The reader is to emphasize the caesuras, to make the commas almost "full stops," and to implicitly add a comma after "Starnbergersee," thereby making "surprise" refer to "rain."

Read in the manner that Bedient describes, the passage does become a kind of "absent-minded" grocery list in which each new item is added as an after-thought: "Summer surprised us"—then, as an aside, as if the line ended with a comma, "coming over the Starnbergersee"—but it surprised us "With a shower of rain." Then, a disjoint list: "we stopped in the colonnade," pause, as if a full stop, "And went on in sunlight," pause, "into the Hofgarten," pause, . . .

This, then, is an instructed reading: an organization of the laic skills of reading that recovers the cogency of the characterization of the passage as consisting of *non sequiturs*.

Bedient's analysis of the opening stanza of *The Waste Land* serves a similar, dual purpose, as do the captions on the photographs in the introductory sociology text. The captions instruct us to view the photographs as indicators of a social phenomenon; Bedient's analysis tells us how we should read the text. By reading the text in that way, the reader finds the cogency of Bedient's analysis. Yet, at the same time, the laic skills of reading—like those of viewing and analyzing the photographs—have been slightly distorted and molded to the analysis. We read the text in such a way as to make the analysis come "true."

V

Earlier, the poetic object was presented as a gestalt in which contextual clues are fitted together to exhibit a precise description of the work of reading its own text. The poetic object reveals the natural analyzability of its text/ reading pair. The Fortunatus poem, the poem by Owen, and the picture poem of Fernbach-Flarsheim in chapter 3 illustrate the endless variety of discoverable ways in which poetic objects can be constructed and the endless variety of discoverable ways in which the laic skills of reading can be configured.

An instructed reading is also a gestalt of reading practice, but different from the poetic object. Bedient's reading of the opening of *The Waste Land* illustrates this.

As we have seen, the summer episode described in *The Waste Land* can be read as an account of a sequence of events—finding shelter from the rain, going into the Hofgarten, having coffee and talking. Against this background, the line in German—approximately, "not Russian, Lithuanian, real German"—appears to be a remembered part of that conversation, and this remembered line is intimately related to further recollections of a more distant past.

In Bedient's reading, the reader is asked to read the events of summer as a list of *non sequiturs*. The fact that this distorts the skills of reading in no way depends on having an alternative reading of the lines; the alternative reading only allows this to be seen more clearly. Let us, instead, stay with Bedient's reading. Given a reading from within which the events of summer appear as *non sequiturs*, the line in German does appear as a more abstract assertion:

> The line in German betrays a petty, in fact false concern with worldly purity, purity of race, national clean and proper boundaries, a concern that, in the context of a poem in which the only clean and proper self is one unbounded before the Divine, is alone sufficient to explain its inclusion.[17]

Quite different from the preceding chatter, the line in German is a new voice that is overheard. Moreover, read in this way, Marie's story of the sled ride does seem to start in the middle of a sentence and to babble on about the events of childhood.

> . . . there are Lithuanians who consider "echt deutsch" anything but Lithuanian. Political temporization? In any case, Marie, all temporization, does not follow from the German with her "And," nor her talk of the fright of sledding that leads, abruptly, to "In the mountains, there you feel free." Marie examines nothing; she only declares, and serially.[18]

The following organization for reading is found: First, there is a morose, flattened voice, reflecting a world of feeling:

> April is the cruellest month, breeding
> Lilacs out of the dead land, mixing

A second voice intrudes and chatters on, drowning out the first voice, pointing to concrete particulars of the world, talking as if the real world consisted only of such concrete things. The lines are to be read as *non sequiturs* and as if a comma were inserted after "Starnbergersee": "Summer surprised us," then a reflection, "coming over the Starnbergersee," pause, because summer surprised us "With a shower of rain"; then a list: "we stopped in the colonnade," pause, almost full stop, "And went on," pause, "in sunlight," almost a full stop, "into the Hofgarten," almost a full stop. . . .

A "wild-card" line follows this passage; a different voice, speaking German, heard above the first two, expresses an abstract proposition involving "purity of race, national clean and proper boundaries."

The voice of Marie comes next—gushing, nonreflective, excited—overheard above the others, caught *in media res* as if she were already speaking. The lines are to be read as if they flowed together without any pause between or within them: "And when we were children, staying at the archduke's, / My cousin's, he took me out on a sled, / And I was frightened. He said, Marie, / . . . ." Finally, Marie says:

> I read, much of the night, and go south in the winter.

This is the way that Bedient reads the text. Previously we noted that he divides the opening stanza into groups of lines, as if actors were claiming the spotlight or as if their speeches were written on pieces of paper and these had been layered one on top of another. Here we see that he has implicitly reshaped the text: the lines of the "second" voice, per Bedient, would be cut up as phrases, each *non sequitur* appearing as a separate line; the line in German might be placed off to the side, only tangentially a part of the text; Marie's account of the sled ride might appear as gushing prose, the lines all strung together, indifferent to their original structure.

Each of Bedient's descriptions of Eliot's lines slightly "adjusts" the laic skills of reading; nevertheless, the descriptions fit together and mutually articulate a structure of reading. The instructed reading is not, in any way, a simple distortion of reading's work; to the contrary, Bedient's reading of the events of summer is supported and amplified by his instructed readings of the other lines. The fundamental pairing of text and reading's work has been skewed; at the same time, the instructed reading still relies upon, and is tied to, those laic skills. Like a poetic object, the instructed reading is a gestalt of the practices of reading, and Bedient's text teaches a method of reading that uncovers that totality.

Bedient's instructed reading provides the substantial grounds of his analysis. That analysis is not irrelevant, for it supplies the good reasons, the accountable reasons, for reading the text in this way. The instructed reading is not simply a reading of the text; it is an objectively accountable reading of the text. The motives for reading the text as Bedient describes become embedded in reading, and the instructed reading, reciprocally, comes to exhibit the cogency of its analysis.

Instructed readings are, in fact, objects. They are objects which distort the laic skills of reading. They do not do this in a crude way, twisting the reading of a text in order to document an abstract argument about it. Bedient's reading is anything but crude; it is an achievement, and an elegant one. Instead, as an object, the instructed reading is an interrelated whole, distorting the laic skills of reading as they are molded within it. It provides a structure for the laic skills of reading that the critical text explicates through its analysis.

VI

Reading, as an activity of the lay community of readers, is a dynamically "paired" and unfolding activity. One part of the pair—conventionally spoken of as the "text"—is an account of how the laic skills of reading need to be organized; the other part of the pair is the ongoing, lived work of reading that finds the descriptiveness of the reading account (the "text") for organizing that work. This is written as a text/reading pair. The achievement of a poetic object is that its reading account becomes available as a precise description of the work of reading that its account requires, a [text/reading] pair. A poetic object takes on the character of a finished, complete, and self-sufficient object.

An instructed reading is also a "reading" of a text, distinct from the critical text that analyzes it. Like a [text/reading] pair, it too is a paired object. It consists of an annotated reading account—denoted as a "text-prime"—and, again, the laic skills of reading. It is a [(text)'/reading] pair. An instructed reading is a completed object; its description in a critical text presupposes a finished, objective reading—a way that the text can or should be read. Yet, at the same time, a [(text)'/reading] pair is also a distortion of the laic skills of reading *simpliciter*; it twists the communally known skills of laic, ordinary reading in order to make its way of reading, and the appropriateness of its annotations, come "true." As an actual reading, an instructed reading offers its pairing of annotated text and reading's work as a reflection and representation of a prior, naturally analyzable text/reading pair.[19]

$$\text{text/reading} \longrightarrow \text{[(text)'/reading]}$$

The transcendentalizing achievement of an instructed reading is a "reversal of arrows": by finding an organization of reading's work that recovers the deeply reasoned text as a method of reading, the [(text)'/reading] pair is seen to make available the poetic object that it projects. Instead of rendering a poetic object, it is seen as revealing the poetic object itself.

$$\text{[text/reading]} \longleftarrow \text{[(text)'/reading]}$$

The annotated text, rather than being produced in isolation from the development of an instructed reading, is built up from within and is part of the method of reading that it seeks to teach. The instructed reading is cultivated as an object: the annotations are pieced together, logical transitions and connectives are supplied, schemes of worldly references are added, all as the means through which the instructed reading comes to stand for and realize an intended [text/reading] pair. The continuities of the instructed reading, its coherence, its schemes of worldly reference, its cogency, its transparency—the orderlinesses of the instructed reading—are transferred to the projected poetic object as *its* continuities, *its* coherence, *its* schemes of worldly reference, *its* cogency, *its* transparencies. In its annotated character, the text stands for, and comes to exhibit, the organization of reading's work that recovers the adequacy of those annotations.

The achievement of an instructed reading is offered as a scheme of substitutions: the annotated text for the common text; cultured, sophisticated reading for reading's laic skills; disciplined analysis for ordinary reasoning; accountable structures of reading for the practical adequacy and natural analyzability of reading's work; the instructed reading for the poetic object. Each repairs the deficiencies of its vulgar partner; each exhibits those deficiencies in and as the achievement of the method of reading that the instructed reading provides. Throughout, reading *simpliciter* sustains and serves an instructed reading: it is the resource, the means, and, in the end, the object of the exegetical enterprise. What else is the claim of an instructed reading other than that any competent, sufficiently tutored reader can read the text in just that way?

VII

Although an instructed reading recognizably distorts ordinary reading, "distortion," perhaps, is not the precise word. Since every reference to "reading" in the critical community is a reference to instructed readings, this "distortion" appears, from within reading *cultura*, to be the condition and the grounds of reading itself. There is, however, one complication.

In any particular case, it is always recognized that the projected substitutions of a cultivated, cultured reading for reading *simpliciter*, of an objectively accountable text for a naturally analyzable text, and of an instructed reading for a poetic object are only projected and not actually realized. No issue of reading is ever settled, in that reading *cultura* always retains its instructed character. From within reading *cultura*, the poetic object is always the promise of an instructed reading—an instructed reading's projected, intended, and horizonal achievement. The instructed character of the reading is always there, within the cultivated readings of the critical community, as a guide. A gap lies between the projected achievement and the instructed reading, and in that gap, critiques, reparative strategies, alternative readings, and new perspectives all find their grounds. Yet, each critique, strategy, and alternative reading reinstitutes this same problem. The problem is recognized, but it is recognized as the condition of reading itself.

The radical character of reading as a text / reading pair lies at the heart of the self-recognized problems of critical interpretation. An instructed reading is tied to the accountable, annotated features of a text, to teaching a method of reading that recovers that accountable text, and to explaining the poetic object which is understood as a prior achievement. The instructed reading, in this way, misses the lived, practical, reflexive character of reading's work, of which such a poetic object, as an achievement, must consist. Although used and, in the end, the object of the critical enterprise, the self-organizing, self-describing, laic skills of reading's work are missed because of the object that an instructed reading must be. The instructed reading presents a reputable, accountable, analyzable structure of reading's work—a documentable coherence, cogency, and consistency of a course of reading. It passes beyond the achievement of reading—the fact, the facticity, and the natural analyzability of reading—as reading's own, distinctive phenomenon. The instructed reading attempts to provide, through its pedagogy of reading, an account of the finished achievement itself.

9.

THE CULTURAL OBJECT

A distortion of reading *simpliciter* pervades an instructed reading as its own gestalt of reading practice. Since instructed readings are the ubiquitous phenomenon of literary criticism, once this distortion is seen, it is seen to fill the critical literature. It is no longer a small thing, the property of a particular, individual reading; it is everywhere. This "distortion" is, in fact, the recognized condition and normal state of critical reading. "Reading" means "reading in this way." The problems of laic reading are seen and known, through instructed readings, as problems of reading *cultura*.

Instructed readings have their origins in ordinary explanations of reading among lay readers. The professional reading, however, depends on the distortion of reading's laic skills. In this dependence, and in its intimate details, an instructed reading is an object of the critical community. It is an "improvement" over lay reading and a self-exhibiting recommendation for the practices of reading as they are known to that community. As cultural objects, instructed readings supply their own ever-present and sustaining grounds for the type of reading which lives within them.

I

Let us consider the first stanza of *The Waste Land* and the beginning of the second in terms of the problems that they cause for ordinary reading.

In the first lines of the opening stanza, April's cruelness is amplified and explained by the statements that lilacs are breeding and that memory and desire, like roots, are being stirred. Winter was preferred—its warmth, the forgetfulness of snow. These perceptions may be unusual; the reader may seek motives for them and seek those motives in the text that follows them. This is a problem of and for laic reading.

The lines following those of April and winter concern the events of a previous summer: people (an "us") were caught in a summer shower; they (now a "we") waited in a colonnade; they had coffee and talked in the Hofgarten. So much is plain. The fact that the "we" of the conversation in the Hofgarten is the "us" that was surprised by summer is unremarkable and unquestioned. Yet, following this is the strange line in German; its intended purpose is not so transparent. A woman says, roughly, that she is not Russian but Lithuanian, a real or genuine German. The attribution of the line to some definite speaker is somewhat problematic, and the difficulty is associated with the significance and import of the line within its surrounding context—that is, for reading *The Waste Land*. The reader must figure out that the people having coffee in the Hofgarten were talking and, in that they were talking, that one thing that was said was the line in German. Although this relationship is generally recognized within reading *simpliciter*, critical commentary has often attributed the line to some different, unknown person whose conversation is overheard by the "we," possibly because of the "uncultured" language of the German speaker. In any case, like the description of April, the line in German should have some bearing and significance for the stanza, and this is not clear.

A more serious and consequential problem of laic reading concerns the referent of "he" in the following lines. The reference may be to the archduke or to one of the "we" who were staying at his residence.

> And when we were children, staying at the archduke's,
> My cousin's, he took me out on a sled,

When "he" is understood as the archduke, the vignette is separated from the preceding events in the Hofgarten, and the scene from childhood seems to concern Marie particularly. The "we" who stayed at the archduke's residence becomes an indeterminate, general reference; it may refer to Marie's family, but it is not directly connected to the events and people in the Hofgarten. The coherence of the scheme of pronominal references becomes problematic; it is no longer clear who the people in the various vignettes are or how they, and the vignettes, are related to each other.

This problem of the referent of "he" is magnified by the lines that follow the sled ride. The "I" that was frightened is read as Marie, and the reader understands that the line that follows—"In the mountains, there you feel free"—is said by her. When she says "there you feel free," "you" is read as Marie's reference to herself. Marie felt "free" in the mountains and now, in contrast, she does not. The primary reference of "free" is to the exhilaration of the sled ride—first the fear, then its release. The reader, however, wants to find the larger significance of the episode. If the "he" of the sled ride is the archduke and, hence, if the sled ride is not directly related to the Hofgarten vignette, the narrative character of the stanza—that it tells a story—appears fragmented. The reader looks for some story that provides continuity for the reading and that makes sense of the growing number of unrelated scenes.

Finally, when the break to a second stanza is encountered and the second stanza begins with a prophetic, rhetorical question directed to "Son of man," the natural analyzability of reading tells the reader that a new voice or speaker is involved. Whether the first stanza in itself is read as the consistent voice of Marie, the reader finds a growing number of different voices. The motives for their introduction and the connections between what they say, as part of the poem as a whole, become problematic.

These aspects of reading and the problems that they engender belong to ordinary reading. Their recognition, and the attempts at their solution, are not foreign to lay readers; readers discuss their readings with each other and try to show how texts can be read. The poetic object, in fact, depends on these problems. It uses the interrelatedness of its contextual clues to form a new precision of reading. The lay reader seeks this precision of reading in the text, and ordinary reading is confounded when it cannot be discovered.

Critical reading addresses such problems as they arise within ordinary reading; critical reading relies on the natural analyzability of ordinary reading. This relationship between reading *cultura* and reading *simpliciter* is part of critical reading's alchemy of reading. However, from within the critical enterprise, both the natural analyzability of reading and the problems that are engendered through it are always seen and understood as part of an instructed reading.

The relevance of Chaucer, the characterization of the opening "voice" and the speaker of the lines, the meaning of the line in German and of the sled ride all address problems that originate in laic reading. At the same time, the particular formulations of these problems and the solutions that are offered are tied to the arts of critical reading and to the critical discourse that has come to surround Eliot's text. Once the opening lines are characterized as "paradoxes," an explanation for their paradoxicalness is sought. Once a confusion in the scheme of pronominal references is seen and a solution given, multiple solutions and nonsolutions can be offered. The line in German can be embedded in different instructed readings, and its significance can be construed in many ways. By examining the work of reading indirectly through instructed readings, and by offering solutions for problems of reading, critical reading makes reading *simpliciter* generally problematic. The natural analyzability of reading comes to ensure nothing about the reading of a text; it is used as a device and resource of critical reading, rather than being examined as the substance of reading itself.

II

Consider the following commentaries on the critical literature that surrounds *The Waste Land:*

> Though much has been written on *The Waste Land*, it will not be difficult to show that most of its critics misconceive entirely the theme and the structure of the poem. There has been little or no attempt to deal with it as a unified whole. F. R. Leavis and F. O. Matthiessen have treated large sections of the poem in detail, and I am obviously indebted to both of them. I believe, however, that Leavis makes some positive errors of interpretation. . . .
> . . .
> The basic symbol used, that of the waste land, is taken of course, from Miss Jessie Weston's *From Ritual to Romance.*[1]

> Almost as soon as it appeared in print, *The Waste Land*'s integrity was questioned. Contemporary reviewers wondered whether its "bright-coloured pieces" formed an "integrated design"[2] or simply a "kaleidoscopic confusion," what Conrad Aiken called an "emotional ensemble" with "a kind of forced unity."[3] Eliot was uneasy enough about whether the pieces cohered that he spoke reassuringly in the Notes about a "plan" and referred readers to Jessie Weston and *The Golden Bough;* it was Eliot himself who thus inspired a half century of misdirected efforts to unify the poem through the wasteland myth.[4]

> All in all, *The Waste Land* has been a goldmine for explicatory critics and, while valuing many of the nuggets they've dug up, we are still left with the problem of what, as poetry, all the unravelled ingenuity adds up to.[5]

> Two issues have continued to remain unresolved in the growing yet often largely repetitious commentary on T. S. Eliot's 1922 masterpiece—the quintessential poem of Anglo-American modernism—*The Waste Land*. One is that of the emotional, intellectual, and cultural disposition of the poem, its stance (if a simplifying figure may be used) toward history, modernity, erotic love, women, the metaphysical. Is it a poem, as many have thought, of despair? Or a poem, as others have believed, of heroically attained salvation? Or, as still others have suggested, of something peculiarly in-between, something baulked? This bewildering range of response—a result, in part, of the tricky reserve, the justifiably profound reticence, of Eliot's poem—characterizes the other major critical issue as well: that of the existence or nonexistence of a single protagonist; of the nature or purpose of the apparent medley of voices. Is it "Eliot" who speaks the

work (or speaks in it)? Or a polyphony of equal voices? Or Tiresias? Or a nameless narrator-protagonist? Or still some other possibility?[6]

The history of discussions of *The Waste Land* can be divided into roughly three dispensations, the first extending from the thirties through the fifties, the second from the sixties to the eighties, and the third beginning in the eighties.
. . .
. . . Calvin Bedient's *He Do the Police in Different Voices: "The Waste Land" and Its Protagonist* (1986) is the one close reading that has appeared [in the recent period].[7] Bedient's study is suggestive, but his controlling assumption that the poem has a single protagonist [see n. 8] is one which, for reasons that will be evident in our study, we cannot accept.

Our book is a return to close reading, a return characterized by an awareness of the scholarship on Eliot's philosophy and also an awareness of the new critical theories.[8]

While some critics propose that the opening stanza of *The Waste Land* is spoken by a single voice, one will see that voice as a persona of Eliot, another as Tiresias, another as Marie, another as a nameless protagonist, and another as the modulation of an opening, oracular voice to the voice of Marie whose concerns specialize and amplify those of the opening lines. One critic proposes that there are separate, distinct voices in the stanza; another claims that these voices are performed by a single protagonist. For one critic, the opening stanza, in part, introduces some of the people who populate the waste land; for another, it elaborates a theme, the attractiveness of death; another emphasizes the mythic cycles of nature, vegetative rites, and the murder and eating of the primal father;[9] still another points to issues concerning the nature of writing and literature. The first lines of the stanza might be read, basically, as trochaic verse; they are described as "a syllable short of iambic pentameter";[10] they are scanned as strong-stress meter, each line containing four stressed beats. Marie is a figure to be despised; she represents a kind of secular estrangement; she is ensnared in the type of relational knowledge that Bradley described. One critic writes that the changes in verb tense are intended to direct attention away from the "story" to the "plot" of the poem; that Eliot may use the pronoun "you" to refer to the protagonist's "me"; and that triads—such as April, winter, and summer—are essential to the structure of the poem as a whole. For one, the line in German is a "wild-card line"; it reflects as well a petty and false concern. For another, Marie quotes the line, and the line itself shows an interest in language and national identity. And for another, the line, if considered as part of the conversation in the Hofgarten, helps indicate "the class and character of the protagonist."[11]

Every aspect of the opening of *The Waste Land* has been read in different ways; every textual detail has been embedded in widely varying courses of instructed readings. Critical commentary builds on critical commentary; old studies are found to be faulted, missing some aspect of reading the text, or only promissory of a fuller analysis; the collected critical writings themselves become a subject of assessment, review, and analysis.[12] No definitive characterization of the literature is possible: each new analysis shapes this situation of reading in a particular way; each offers another analysis into the collection.

Among and between all these instructed readings, the critical literature offers a phenomenon that belongs peculiarly to the critical community. Critical writings reflect the state of art concerning the reading of a particular text; they generate a situation of inquiry into its reading.[13] The formulation of this situation is part of the same critical domain and contributes to this state of reading. For members of the community who produce critical studies, who seek to advance the art of reading *The Waste Land*, the situation of inquiry surrounding the text provides the essential background for reading the poem.

A new reading never arises in isolation, nor can the merits of a new reading be disengaged from the communal arts of reading *cultura* or from the current state of professional inquiry. This would deny the grounds, conditions, and circumstances of the new reading—that the critical literature has missed something about the reading of the text and, specifically, that it has missed something relevant to the situation of inquiry itself.

III

Demonstrably, by reference to the situation of professional inquiry into the reading of any particular text, the ordinary, laic skills of reading provide insufficient grounds for asserting the accountable structures of reading that text. Every reference to a text, to what a text says, to an interpretation, to meaning, to grammatical structure, to rhetorical figures, to prosody, is a reference to an instructed reading of a text. Ordinary reading is revealed as something indeterminate and lacking authority, explicated, clarified, and understood only through its cultivation and culturation within an instructed reading. What it means to "read" the opening stanza of *The Waste Land* is no longer clear except as an instructed reading of that stanza.

The following discussion of the opening stanza of *The Waste Land* is taken from Brooker and Bentley's book *Reading "The Waste Land."*[14]

Two perspectives exist and contend within Marie's mind. Her present in the waste land involves a partially successful evasion of natural cycles, but her past, still present in memory, includes an acceptance of circularity as the form of straight-line growth. "And down we went," she says, recalling a descent in winter which constituted an ascent beyond fear to freedom. As a child, Marie had lived in a largely nondualistic world in which she accepted contradictions because she did not perceive them as contradictions; as an adult, she lives in a world of intolerable paradoxes created by her compulsion to perceive up and down, fear and security, circular and straight, as contraries. She sees paradoxes as openings onto vistas of chaos. Like all inhabitants of the waste land, she interprets April as cruel because it breeds life from death, because it brings endless circularity and unavoidable paradox. The opening voice suggests that Marie's interpretation issues from mixing memory and desire, past and future. Memory is vividly presented in the image of a childhood experience, but desire is left vague. Marie is portrayed as stretched between a past which was in special ways unconscious and carefree and a future which may in some way correspond to that childhood condition. She perceives the dualistic and paradoxical present as cruel because, in remembering the past and intuiting the future, she is left with a vacuum in the present moment, an absence in the middle of her life.

In Bradley's terms, Marie is trapped in relational knowledge. . . .

The first indication that the skills of ordinary reading have been skewed is the extraction of the line in German. The passage above does not mention this line; it is removed and discussed separately. Elsewhere, Brooker and Bentley claim that the line is quoted by Marie, and that it shows a concern, either of Eliot or of Marie, "with language and national identity,"[15] a claim having little to do with the above analysis. The second indication that reading has been skewed lies in Brooker and Bentley's reading of the stanza's first two lines. Brooker and Bentley ask us to read "April is the cruellest month, breeding / Lilacs out of the dead land, mixing . . ." as saying that April "breeds life from death." The lines are to be read as a rhetorical figure where lilacs stand for life and dead land represents death. Moreover, as spring follows winter, so winter will eventually follow spring; as life breeds from death, so death will follow life. By ruing the coming of spring, per Brooker and Bentley, the speaker of the lines is actually seeking to deny the paradoxes and endless circularity of life.

To get further access to Brooker and Bentley's reading, the opening lines of *The Waste Land* need to be re-examined. These lines indicate, at least in part, that the cruelty of April involves memories that are stirred like dull roots. Each successive scene of the stanza—winter, summer, the sled ride—is a memory of an increasingly remote past. The sled ride is the last such memory;

it is the most dramatic, and it is the one from which Marie immediately distances herself. Therein, the sled ride might be seen as the realization of the memories that the opening lines described as being stirred, and which the speaker of the lines seeks to avoid.

> And when we were children, staying at the archduke's,
> My cousin's, he took me out on a sled,
> And I was frightened. He said, Marie,
> Marie, hold on tight. And down we went.
> In the mountains, there you feel free.

On this basis, Brooker and Bentley write that "memory is vividly presented in the image of a childhood experience, but desire is left vague."

For the last line of the quoted passage from *The Waste Land*, Brooker and Bentley read the reference to the mountains as, in the first instance, a reference to the sled ride; Marie's use of "you" is understood as a reference to herself. Marie felt "free" in the mountains, and now, through the contrast, she does not. So much is given from within reading *simpliciter*. Brooker and Bentley, however, treat the sled episode much as they do the opening lines concerning April. The opening lines are read as an instance of a general condition—the paradoxes and circularities of life. Similarly, the sled ride is read as an indicator of a general state: being frightened and feeling free no longer concern the sledding episode in itself, but are reflections of fear and freedom in general, another pair of contradictory elements of life. The grounds for this interpretation lie within reading *simpliciter*, for Marie's troubles do not concern just the sled ride; the sled ride is a reflection or embodiment of them. Brooker and Bentley go beyond the sled ride as a revelation of these troubles, considering it in terms of freedom and fear as philosophical abstractions.

> "And down we went," she says, recalling a descent in winter which consti-
> tuted an ascent beyond fear to freedom. As a child, Marie had lived in a largely
> nondualistic world in which she accepted contradictions because she did not
> perceive them as contradictions; as an adult, she lives in a world of intolerable
> paradoxes created by her compulsion to perceive up and down, fear and
> security, circular and straight, as contraries.

In Marie's childhood, fear and freedom were not antagonistic and paradoxical; opposites were not seen in a dualistic fashion. Both the breeding of lilacs out of dead land and the contrast of fear and freedom are seen as indicators of the same general, natural condition, viewed differently by Marie at different times in her life.

These characterizations of the opening lines and the sled ride reinforce one another. In doing so, they also articulate another feature of Brooker and Bentley's reading. If the stanza is read as a continuous narrative, the story has dramatic tension. The cruelty of April is due, in part, to the memories that spring occasions; winter was better because these memories were forgotten. What, then, does Marie not want to recognize or recall?

> Marie is portrayed as stretched between a past which was in special ways unconscious and carefree and a future which may in some way correspond to that childhood condition. She perceives the dualistic and paradoxical present as cruel because, in remembering the past and intuiting the future, she is left with a vacuum in the present moment, an absence in the middle of her life.

The avoidance of cyclic nature is balanced with a previous time of its acceptance, and the dramatic aspect of the narrative is explicated. The benefits of winter expressed in Eliot's lines and the relevance of Marie's going south in winter are clarified and explained, as Brooker and Bentley write, as "a partially successful evasion of natural cycles." In her present life, Marie lives with this partial evasion, whereas in the past she accepted "circularity as the form of straight-line growth."

Why have Brooker and Bentley written their commentary as they have? The authors' discovery is an instructed reading, and their critical text analyzes that reading as a pedagogy of it.

Brooker and Bentley's critical text analyzes this reading, and in passages unquoted here, they elaborate that reading's significance and accountability. In that Brooker and Bentley's reading emerges, in part, from considerations of problems of laic reading, laic reading helps to provide the grounds for it. In that the text can be "read" this way, the laic skills of reading are essential to it and help ensure that it is a reading. Yet, in detail, ordinary reading is being forced in an unnatural manner. The lines of Eliot's text do not "say" any of what Brooker and Bentley say exactly.

If the details of Brooker and Bentley's analysis are compared with the text of *The Waste Land*, each of the characterizations of the lines is suspect. It is not clear that the central contrast is between childhood and present age; that paradox and endless circularity are those things which are painful; that memories "stretch" Marie between past and present; that reified "fear" and "freedom" are the essential aspects of the sled episode. At the same time, it is not clear that the text does not "say" this. Nor that Brooker and Bentley actually say what they have been presented as saying. Reading, as an activity, has become indefinite in its specifics.

Three aspects of Brooker and Bentley's reading recommend themselves, however. First, their reading addresses the critical situation of inquiry. Brooker and Bentley solve problems for the discipline and reading *cultura:* the relevance of critical theory, the connection between *The Waste Land* and Bradley's philosophy, the nature and continuity of the first stanza and its speaker or speakers, the meaning of the "paradoxes" and the cruelty of April, the explanation of Marie's going south in the winter, the relevance of the stanza to the poem as a whole, and to Eliot's work more generally—although "love" is not explicated as part of their reading, Brooker and Bentley gently twist their own reading to this point. One way for Marie to escape the dualisms of relational knowledge would be through love,[16] thus:

> In Eliot's work, from beginning to end, waste lands are related to failures of love,[17] to failures of individuals to transcend their separate spheres and become complements in a comprehensive and mutually nourishing unity. But Marie, Eliot suggests, is as incapable of love as of mythic consciousness and will never escape from her trap, will always experience April as cruel.[18]

Second, Brooker and Bentley's reading is a "new" reading of the text: in itself and as part of a reading of *The Waste Land* in its entirety, it is not a familiar reading that already belongs to the critical literature. The "newness" of the reading is the newness of the solution it offers for the problems of the critical situation of inquiry. The problems of reading that Brooker and Bentley address are not alien to reading *simpliciter,* but those problems, and reading *simpliciter,* have been reconfigured from within their instructed reading.

The third and most important recommendation for Brooker and Bentley's reading is its achievement: the opening stanza of *The Waste Land* can be "read" in a manner that makes their analysis a cogent description of that reading. Brooker and Bentley's reading *is* a "reading" of the text, and their critical text stands proxy for the discovered reading that it analyzes. Through their "reading," reading is revealed as an instructed reading, and its associated text is revealed as a deeply reasoned text, a text which evinces the accountable structures of how it should be read, with good and sensible reasons for reading it in that manner.

IV

Proposing to a physicist that the manner in which he or she manipulates an experimental apparatus determines the properties of a phenomenon, while true, is trivialized for the physicist by the demonstrable achievement of those practices—the revealed, propertied, physical object.[19] Similarly, an instructed reading is embedded in and depends on the arts of reading as they are practiced within the critical disciplines. Yet that dependence is trivialized by its own achievement.

Within an instructed reading, the ordinary skills and natural analyzability of reading have been, at every turn, rearticulated, respecified, problematized, and distorted. Yet, in this context, the instructed reading has one other central feature. As its achievement, it itself comes to show what the laic skills of reading could be. They are the skills of reading required to recover that instructed reading as that particular [(text)'/reading] pair. When, and if, a reader finds Brooker and Bentley's reading of the opening stanza, or Bedient's, or Brooks's, or Smith's, the reader finds that the text could be read in the manner that each of them analyzes, that the laic skills of reading could be organized to read the text in that way. The literary community knows reading in this way, and for that community, instructed readings demonstrate the structures of reading's prosaic work.

For the literary community, an instructed reading is a discovery about reading's work; it is a discovery of what reading could look like and what it could be. Talk of a "distortion" of reading or of the essential disciplinarity of the community's practices of reading—other than as the grounds for new instructed readings—is trivialized by the witnessed achievements of the discipline. An instructed reading shows that a text can be read in the manner which the critical text describes. Therein, the critical enterprise maintains its real-world, material interests: that it is about reading, not theoretically, not imaginatively, but as the real project that its own literature exhibitably and accountably shows.

The details of a text that emerge from within an instructed reading are those details that are specifically relevant to the instructed reading—the relevance of Chaucer, the paradoxical character of the opening lines, the cyclic nature of the seasons, the problematic continuity of a single voice, the meaning of the sled episode. The achievement of an instructed reading is seen against the background of other instructed readings and their associated annotated texts. Against this background, the instructed reading emerges as an achievement. An instructed reading needs to show a new organization of reading's work; it needs to rework the multiply annotated text. It addresses the situation of inquiry of which it is a part. For the members of the literary community that an instructed reading collects, its achievement is a discovery about reading's work—a discovery which is anonymous as to authorship, a property of the text, a discovery for any competent reader to see. But in its distortion of reading *simpliciter* and in the relevance of its details to the professional situation of inquiry, the instructed reading is also a discovery of the community and, recognizably, a product of it. It is, in fact, a cultural object.

10.

A FAMILY ROMANCE

The distortion of reading in an instructed reading, the pervasiveness of that distortion, the embeddedness of an instructed reading in a professional situation of inquiry, and the relationship between an instructed reading and a surrounding culture of reading are all aspects of critical reading. The picture is made whole by the intrinsic motives that drive that culture and animate a critic's work.

For the sociologist, sociology is about the real society; for the psychologist, psychology is about the properties of the mind; and for the literary critic, criticism is about the work of reading "really." The embeddedness of practitioners' work within the practices of the disciplines allow the practitioner to see beyond those practices to the real-worldly objects that animate the profession. The real society, the mind, reading-really are the "things" that concern the disciplines.

I

In introductory textbooks on sociology, sociology is defined as the scientific study of society. "Society" is used to refer to the ordinary, familiar world of practical action and reasoning. Society is the communal world in which the members of a society engage in concerted action; it is the communal world that consists of just those concerted actions. Through and as those concerted actions, members of society create and recreate, exhibit and manage, normalize and transform the society and its familiar appearances. Sociology treats the structures of social action: what they are; how they are produced and maintained; how they are modified and changed; how they are analyzed, and how they are made analyzable, by the members of society. Sociology concerns the methods that members of society use for creating and managing the familiar society, and the methods that are appropriate for studying and theorizing about those methods.

100

As there are endless variations on the specific meaning of each of these themes, there are endless variations on the meaning of the word "scientific." In sociology, the predominant formulation of "science" is that a researcher develops testable hypotheses about the structures of social action. Such hypotheses involve "concepts" which are operationalized so that "data" can be collected. Data are collected in a manner that appears objective and unbiased, so that the results of a study seem capable of replication. Through the examination of the relationship between the data and the hypotheses, an enriched understanding of the nature of society is obtained, often expressed in terms of conclusions or further hypotheses.

This sketch provides one formulation of "science" in sociology. It also conceals the deeper concern that lies behind the word. When it is said that sociology is the scientific study of society, "scientific" emphasizes the interest of sociologists in the "real," as opposed to a "theorized" or "imagined," society. "Society" is understood as the looks, sounds, actions, and reasoning of the familiar social world. Independently of the manner in which it is expressed, the locus of sociological concern is to speak about and investigate this real society. The term "science" can be construed in different ways and even rejected; if the idea of consulting the material appearances of the real society is lost, "sociology," whatever it is, becomes something different.

Although the abiding interest in sociology is in the real society, the appearances of the real society are subject to a distortion similar to that of reading by professional literary critics. An example is provided by a particular ensemble of five photographs displayed together on a page in an introductory sociology text.[1] The ensemble occurs as part of a discussion of collective behavior and crowds.

Of the five photographs in the ensemble, the one in the upper left corner shows people seated in small groups on the steps of a building. The caption reads:

> Casual crowds gather in pleasant public places. In New York City, a favorite spot is the steps of the Public Library.

The upper right photograph contains a hearse with two priests standing beside it, pallbearers carrying a coffin, and a few other people. The caption says:

> Conventional crowds, such as people attending a funeral, typically act according to well-defined cultural norms.

The center photograph is of young people in bleachers, standing and cheering, some with their hands raised. The bottom left corner of the ensemble is a picture of a large political demonstration; in the bottom right photograph, bodies are lying on the ground with people looking at them and milling around them. The respective captions read:

> Expressive crowds can often be found at sports events. American fans are almost as active as the athletes on the playing field.

> Protest crowds played an important part in bringing down the Marcos regime in the Philippines in 1986.

> Soccer fans at the 1985 European Cup finals in Brussels turned into a violent acting crowd. Before police were able to restore order, thirty-eight people had died.

Each of the photographs is described through its associated caption as representing a different type of crowd, the last photograph indirectly. Yet at least four of the five pictures present problems in terms of those captions. In the photograph of the people on the steps of the library, the individual groupings of people seem to dominate rather than their anonymous collectivity as a whole; they are simply people sitting outside, in small groups of "friends." The number of people in the funeral scene seems peculiarly small, a total of eleven; given just the photograph, the participants seem to constitute a relatively small gathering. The people in the bleachers may not be part of a massive crowd: the photograph looks to be cropped, and the people that we see may be all that there was of a small bleacher at a high-school pep rally. Why the people depicted in the aftermath of crowd violence do not themselves constitute a crowd is not clear.

The problem with the photographs is not peculiar to these photographs, nor can it be fixed by using others. It is not clear why people at the funeral, no matter how large, are not "expressive" or why the scenes are not all examples of "acting" crowds. The captions try to make available a phenomenon not in any photograph—the inherent difference and distinguishability of different collectivities of people. If all the photographs depicted immense numbers of people, the pedagogical purpose of the ensemble would be hindered: the sheer size of the "crowds," rather than the claimed variations between them, would be their shared, predominant feature.

What all the pictures, separately and together, do suggest is the concerted character of action among people who, as a specific feature of their actions, remain relatively anonymous to each other. People do things together—sit in identifiable groups, maintain a general demeanor, cheer, position their bodies and walk, stampede—without making it a matter of recognized interpersonal interaction. Probably none of the people in the picture discussed among themselves the structure of their groupings or actions; it would make little difference if some of them had. This is what underlies the idea of "collective behavior."

The captions associated with the photographs depend on this but do not articulate it. They do not directly analyze the "crowdness" of each of the depicted scenes. Instead, the captions develop an abstract idea of a crowd through the diversity of its possible effacements as "casual" crowds, "conventional" crowds, "expressive" crowds, "protest" crowds, and "acting" crowds. While the distinctions make some ordinary sense, they are references to a professional literature for which such distinctions are technical matters. Our own ability to find the relevance of and to use such descriptions is then, in a sense, turned against us; the plausibility of the descriptions becomes evidence for something that is not seen. The problematic analyzability of the ordinary, familiar society has been reformulated in terms of the evidence that society offers for an abstract analysis of it; the depicted scenes become token illustrations of the vitality of that abstract analysis.

The captioned photographs are, in fact, a pedagogy of the "real." The difficulties involved in analyzing these particular photographs—how they are crowds and what they show about "crowds"—are to be excused in light of the analysis in which they are embedded. The depicted scenes are indicators of the "real" structures of crowd behavior, and the realness of society comes to lie in the cogency of its analysis. Even though sociology is directed to real-world studies of the ordinary society, the "real" society has been mystified; the reality of the real society has become the affair of a community of sociologists, and the authority for an analysis of the society comes to reside within professional practice.

In a similar manner, literary criticism is directed to the study of the "real." It takes reading as its fundamental phenomenon and seeks to understand the way in which our society reads. If literary criticism is not about how we can or should or might or actually do read particular texts, the coherence of the discipline and the worldliness of the discipline's project are lost. If critical writings do not return us, in one way or another, to a concern with reading and to a concern with the reading of particular texts, literary criticism ceases to be literary criticism. Criticism loses the materiality of its interests and is, then, seemingly about everything and about nothing.

The project of literary criticism is to understand "reading," really, as a worldly and communally available phenomenon. However, as sociology's concern with the real society refers to the society as it is available from within the discipline, "reading" for the critical community refers to the phenomenon of reading as it is available to that community. Reading is the type of reading that the community does, and evidently, within that community, that type of reading is the state, condition, and reality of reading itself.

II

Let us consider the beginning of the second stanza of *The Waste Land*. Following the sledding episode and Marie's distancing herself from it, the lines describe a bleak terrain. Written in the oracular tone of the biblical prophets, they begin with a rhetorical question that invites the listener into an unexplicated metaphor about his or her present condition:

> What are the roots that clutch, what branches grow
> Out of this stony rubbish? Son of man,
> You cannot say, or guess, for you know only

We hear the demanding voice of the prophet before us. The second line (line 20 of *The Waste Land*) ends not as a question to be answered but as a call to and claim on the listener: "Son of man," listen to me, I will tell you. The question is an opening for the explication that follows it, except, as is often the case in biblical prophecy, the lines that follow do not explain the metaphor. Here, lines 22–24 explain why, in fact, the listener cannot answer the question.

"Son of man" is a rhetorical device: it asks the listener to see himself or herself in terms of a generality—that the listener is a "Son of man"—and, therein, that what is to be depicted is the general condition of one who is a "Son of man." In lines that follow, the speaker tells and, thereby, claims—in essence—what the listener knows of and about the world. It is a desolate landscape. The world is described in concrete terms, but again, each of the images and all of them together are unexplicated. They are metaphors for what the listener knows of this world, rendering the listener incapable of answering the initial question.

A glimmer of hope follows this description, added to line 24 almost as a reflective afterthought. As with the other images, the "dry stone" offers no lightening of the oppression:

> And the dry stone no sound of water. Only

"Only" there may be something more; some revelation may be possible; listen further.

The prophetic invitation is then made: what I, the speaker, have told you is the world that you know; yet . . .

> And the dry stone no sound of water. Only
> There is shadow under this red rock,
> (Come in under the shadow of this red rock),

If the listener will follow the prophet, some illumination may be gained, some truth revealed.

What truth? The symbolic meaning of this civilization or culture in ruins? No, what is revealed is something more fearful than death, described metaphorically in a manner reminiscent of the Sphinx's riddle (lines 28–29). What is feared is that there is no revelation, that there is no deeper meaning to this life; from dust to dust and nothing more.

> I will show you fear in a handful of dust.

The reader must read the opening of the second stanza to see beyond the synopsis and recover the immediacy, drama, and force of the lines as an actual course of literal reading. Primacy is given to the actual reading of the lines: the lines can be read in this way; reading them in this manner provides the grounds for offering instruction in that reading. Another voice from Eliot's *The Waste Land* is heard, and the poetic achievement, for some, is that Eliot could produce a text that reads like this.

III

The preceding reading sets in relief the critical texts that follow. These texts analyze how the opening of the second stanza of *The Waste Land* can be read. They represent studies of the work of reading-really. Through them, "reading-really" becomes available as a phenomenon both of the community and for the community of literary critics. In the following quotation, the critic has re-presented the line structure of *The Waste Land*. The bracketed words of *The Waste Land* are not present in the critic's text.

> The first part of "The Burial of the Dead" introduces this theme [that "men dislike to be roused from their death-in-life"] through a sort of reverie on the part of the protagonist. . . . The reverie is resumed with line 19.

> What are the roots that clutch, what branches grow
> Out of this stony rubbish? [Son of man,]

The protagonist answers for himself:

> [Out of this stony rubbish?] Son of man,
> You cannot say, or guess, for you know only
> A heap of broken images, where the sun beats,
> And the dead tree gives no shelter, the cricket no relief,
> And the dry stone no sound of water. [Only]

In this passage there are references to Ezekiel and to Ecclesiastes, and these references indicate what it is that men no longer know: The passage referred to in Ezekiel 2, pictures a world thoroughly secularized:

> 1. And he said unto me, Son of man, stand upon thy feet, and I will speak unto thee.
> 2. And the spirit entered into me when he spake unto me, and set me upon my feet, that I heard him that spake unto me.
> 3. And he said unto me, Son of man, I send thee to the children of Israel, to a rebellious nation that hath rebelled against me: they and their fathers have transgressed against me, even unto this very day.[2]

In this analysis, the idea that someone is asking a nonrhetorical question and then "answers for himself" vitiates the prophetic and biblical character of the lines. It is true that a world in which broken images are only broken images and where a dry stone is only a dry stone is a world without a divine interpretation—a secularized world. Yet the lines from Ezekiel are not particularly illuminating. The analysis emphasizes the thematic unity of *The Waste Land* and its relationship to a single protagonist. When Eliot's text is inspected to find, precisely, how its words should be read, the analysis loses coherence; it is indefinite and vague in its particulars and, at best, only suggestive.

The next analysis tries to resolve the ambiguities of prophetic speech through a scheme of correspondences, thus attempting to illuminate *The Waste Land* as "a reworking of the themes of the prophetic writings of the Old and New Testaments."[3]

> To turn then to Eliot's poem is to find oneself on surprisingly familiar ground. There is the same wasteland, the same desolate city, the same faithless woman and futile king [as in the Book of Jeremiah]. As for the land:[4]

> What are the roots that clutch, what branches grow
> . . .
> I will show you fear in a handful of dust.

> The allusions are at once apparent. What indeed is the root that clutches and the branch that grows from stony rubbish but the Servant of God described by Deutero-Isaiah:

> For he grew up before him like a young plant,
> and like a root out of dry ground. . . . (Is. 53:2)

And what is he but the Righteous Branch (Jer. 23:5) which would be raised up out of David? Or he might be designated as "Son of man," a title which belongs, in one sense, to any man. It was used by Ezekiel for his own designation as God's prophet and by the author of the Book of Daniel as the name of the divine hero of the apocalypse, and Christ then took it as his own peculiar title.

Similarly with the "red rock." ("Come in under the shadow of this red rock"). In the same context with the "handful of dust," it recalls the lines from Isaiah:

> Enter into the rock,
> and hide in the dust
> from before the terror of the Lord. . . . (Is. 2:10)

Yet what rock will hide men in safety, unless the Lord himself, who is "a shelter from the storm and a shade from the heat" (Is. 25:4); "an everlasting rock" (Is. 26:4); "the Rock of your refuge" (Is. 17:10). If the passage in Eliot's poem appears on the face of it more ominous than reassuring, there is the same ambivalent tone in the prophetic sources. In Jeremiah, God is enemy as well as saviour. So here in Isaiah: he is a "rock of stumbling" as well as the rock of refuge. The "LORD of hosts . . . let him be your dread. And he will become a sanctuary, and a stone of offence, and a rock of stumbling to both houses of Israel, a trap and a snare to the inhabitants of Jerusalem" (Is. 8:13–14). The ambivalence in the prophet's attitude comes from his knowledge that God alone controls the destiny of Israel: it is he who condemns and he who delivers from condemnation. If the people would only recognize the author of their misfortune, they would find at the same time their source of confidence and rescue. May it not be that this applies in Eliot's wasteland also?

One is led at this point to identify the "something different from either / Your shadow at morning striding behind you / Or your shadow at evening rising to meet you" (that is, to take a hint from the cadence that suggests Eccles. 12, "something to alter one's perspective from one's sense of self-sufficiency in youth, and one's sense of futility in old age"). The "something different" must surely be the fear of the Lord on the part of man, the reverence for the Creator on the part of the creature whom he has made from a "handful of dust." ("I will show you something different, . . . I will show you fear in a handful of dust.") The placing of this phrase, "handful of dust," in the passage from the poem puts it in line with "stony rubbish," "a heap of broken images," and "dry stone." These in turn recall the phrases used by the prophets to describe the arid spiritual soil of God's people Israel, given over to exploitation and idolatry: "the heap of ruins of your idols," "wilderness," "desolation," "heart of stone." Rightfully men fear God, not only because they are his creatures, but because they are wayward and unjust while he is eminently righteous, and they stand under his condemnation.[5]

The allusions are anything but "apparent." Why should "roots that clutch" be the "Servant of God"? Why should "Son of man" be Christ? Why the "red rock" the Lord? And why "something different" fear of the Lord? In a manner similar to the previous analysis, biblical quotations are juxtaposed with Eliot's text in the hope that they will illuminate each other. How the skills of reading should be organized to actually read the text is far from clear.

A third example of an analysis of this same passage is the following:

> In the passage under discussion, the son of man is caught, like Marie and like the wounded king, in relational experience. The unity of immediate experi- ence, of childhood, of youthful vigor, has obviously passed, and the unity on a higher plane, which comes with transcendent experience, with mythic imagina- tion, or with restored health, has not been achieved. The wound has been inflicted, and the curse is everywhere evident in this waste land of stony rub- bish, broken images, dead trees, dry stones, this land of unrelieved heat and merciless light. The term "son of man" is a conventional designation of Christ, used throughout the Bible. In fact, Christ refers to himself some eighty times in the Gospels as the son of man. In the context of Eliot's reliance upon Frazer's *Golden Bough* and other anthropological studies in the history of religion, it should also be noted that Christ, like the Fisher King, Osiris, Adonis, Attis, and countless others, is a manifestation of the same mythic impulse toward insuring the fertility of the earth by ritualistically killing heroes and kings. The Christ of this intermediate state of awareness (awareness of disjunction between him- self and his people), the Christ of the waste land of stony rubbish, would be the smitten pre-Resurrection Christ. The speaker who addresses Christ is not named, but as one who appears in a waste land and asks questions of a wounded god-king, he is a formal equivalent of Perceval, the questing knight who presents questions, the answers to which can lift the curse. Or he may be thought of as a formal opposite, for Perceval asks questions he knows can be answered, whereas this speaker asks questions he knows cannot be answered. A figure from one myth, Perceval, asks questions of a figure from another myth, Christ, and the insistence that no direct answer can be conceived is an indication that mythic solutions are no longer possible. The prison of relational (intellec- tual, dualistic) experience has snapped shut, with consequences that are power- fully suggested in this verse paragraph.
>
> Consider, further, that Christ is the "son of man" only in one of his manifestations. He is also the son of God. In Hegelian terms, he is not an analytic either/or figure but a synthetic both/and figure. This means that the central person in Christian culture is a hypostatic union of finite man in time and infinite god out of time. A consideration of Christ must lead to this simultaneity of time and timelessness, and thus, if faith is achieved (more precisely, if the incarnation is accepted), it will be an achievement of the transcendence of paradox in which a both/and arrangement of contraries will be as obvious and clear as it is, in relational terms, absurd. For these reasons, it follows that the address to the son of man by the anti-Perceval is a result of having separated his human and divine natures, of having isolated his finitude and earthly identity from his infinite nature. The address by the anti-Perceval

suggests, in fact, that Christ has no divine nature. He who was thought a god is only a man trapped in a system of relations. The episode can now be read (one of several possible readings at this point) as a comment on the effect of relational consciousness on the religious (for the West, Christian) experience. The opposite of Perceval asks all gods, who within the relational modern consciousness are only anthropological curiosities, questions he knows they cannot answer. Their realms are heaps of broken images, contingent bundles of mere qualities, where light, a conventional sign of (paradoxically) both secular and divine knowledge, prevents knowledge of any metaphysical substance within those bundles of qualities. The hope of drawing water from the rock, substance from matter, as Moses did, is explicitly denied. One hope, however, remains: the red rock. The rock is a biblical and Christian symbol of the church; the red rock is a Frazerian symbol of the place of bloody sacrifice. Eliot's red rock, pulling in these associations, provides a shadow, a conventional sign of illusion, from which the one truth that is not illusion can be understood, fear in a handful of dust. Most important, the shadow is known to be a shadow, the illusions offered by the church are known to be illusions, but they nevertheless provide a point from which a special certitude can be experienced, the certitude of dread.[6]

If reading is understood in terms of the discovered orderlinesses of the work of reading a particular text, and if the explication of reading is understood as the elucidation of a text's own description of reading's work, the above exegeses say very little about actually reading the second stanza of *The Waste Land*. To put the matter more plainly, if "reading" is understood as the community of lay readers practically understands it, these texts say almost nothing, and nothing directly, about reading *The Waste Land*. What they do say is found only through the kindest of interpretations.

Setting these critical texts next to one another reveals a diametrically opposed perspective. If the literary community has misconstrued and mystified the laic skills of reading, its members have not done so individually, but as a community. Nor is that misconstruing and mystification discrete and identifiable in isolated instances. The transmutation of reading *simpliciter* is ubiquitous throughout the discipline, part of a pervasive set of practices through which the arts of reading are professionally analyzed and made accountable.

Rather than illustrating the faulted character of the critical enterprise, the previous analyses reveal a situation of professional inquiry in which these critical texts are serious studies of the reading of *The Waste Land*. It is a situation of inquiry of which each of the above readings is a part; it is a situation of inquiry which the readings, together, help generate and sustain. The readings reflect a culture in which it is appropriate to analyze reading in this way and in which such analyses are analyses of the material-specific work of reading-really. Reading is mystified and then, as the projected achievement of an analysis, identified with the practices of critical reading.

For the critical community, however, these texts are speaking of reading-really. That they are is a phenomenon of the community of critics. Reading-really—the reading of *The Waste Land*, for example—has become and is the romance of the discipline. The mystification of reading *simpliciter* is part of this romance. Each new analysis tries to say better what this thing "reading-really" is—how, in fact, *The Waste Land* should be read. As all references to reading become references to how the community reads, "reading-really" has become the affair of the community—its ever-projected, eventual, if nowhere yet attained achievement.

IV

The collection of instructed readings of a particular text provides the recognized grounds for, and the authority that sustains, both this type of reading and the community of readers who read in this way. Each new critical reading sustains, elaborates, and reinstitutes a condition of reading; each instructed reading seeks reading-really as its projected achievement. That the opening of the second stanza of *The Waste Land* is part of a reverie depicting the secularization of the world, that Perceval is asking a question of Christ, and that the "roots that clutch" are the Servant of God are all seen as meritorious contributions to a situation of inquiry regarding reading, giving new or finer nuances to the reading of *The Waste Land*.

"Reading"—reading-really—has become a confusing mess for outsiders of the critical community. Not so for the critical community. The mystery of reading pervades each instructed reading and each critical text; it is a mystery essential to the project of finding reading-really, and it is a mystery of the critic's and the community's own practices of reading.

That critical analysis concerns reading-really depends on the fact that the reading practices of the critical community belong to the community, that "reading" is done and understood in the manner of the community, and that each critical analysis comes to exhibit the practices of reading that are proper and demonstrably adequate for that community. Those practices of reading fundamentally concern, reflect, and, in an oblique manner, are about the community's own practices of reading. The community's practices of reading exhibit, to the community, that such reading is about reading "really."

In this unavoidable, irreparable, but non-self-conscious way, instructed readings turn back on and come to be about themselves; they come to concern a collection of instructed readings and the practices of finding and teaching instructed readings. In this peculiar and indirect way, literary criticism is about the practices of literary criticism, and professional reading is about the practices of professional reading. Reading-really is the romance of this community and, like all romances, it is sustained and made vital by its participants.

11.

AN ALCHEMY OF PRACTICE

Poets and critics piece together the practices of their communities. Their knowledge is an alchemical knowledge; they mold their practices and, hence, those of their communities into sculpted, social objects. Their creations—poetic objects and instructed readings—are rediscoveries and recreations of these communities, shaping the communities' practices into something new, yet reinstituting and celebrating the community at the same time. Poetic objects and instructed readings are cultural achievements, and as cultural achievements, they come to reveal the alchemical arts of their makers.

I

At first, a "poem" may seem to be a "poem" because it has the properties of "poems." Poems are gathered together in collections—metaphysical poetry, satire, *vers libre*—and discussed as members of such collections. General properties are abstracted from poems, and a poem is an object which possesses those properties.

Such considerations distract attention from the experience of the poetic object. To speak of "poems" is to avoid the problems of poetry—that a poetic object exhibits its poetry in its uniqueness as that particular, witnessed object, in and as the distinctive discovery of reading's work that it reveals. A poetic object does "something" to, and from within, the activity of reading. This achievement offers the poetic object as a "poem," not the other way around. The witnessed achievement of a poetic object provides the basis for, yet is different from, the abstract properties of a "poem."

Computer programming, a field seemingly far removed from poetry, makes this contrast between witnessed achievement and abstract properties more dramatic. Computer algorithms are considered to be algorithms because they have the general properties that algorithms should have. Nothing seems more assured, yet nothing is further from the truth. A specific algorithm has the general properties of all algorithms because of its own, witnessed, idiosyncratic achievement.

The similarity between algorithms and poetic objects can be used to advantage. By taking the foreign object—the practical algorithm—and making it familiar, we provide grounds for taking the familiar object—the poetic object—and making it strange. Both objects are achievements of the cultural practices in which they are embedded.

II

Let us consider the problem of whether a random list of names can be rearranged in alphabetical order in an algorithmic, or strictly mechanical, fashion. Is it possible to describe a procedure for sorting names alphabetically that requires only that the procedure be followed explicitly?

It would seem that a definition of an algorithm is needed. The following informal definition is similar to characterizations that are given in beginning courses in computer science.[1]

1. An algorithm solves a problem.
2. It solves the problem by giving a list of instructions for that problem's solution.
3. The instructions
   a) are finite in number,
   b) are unambiguous as to the actions that they describe,
   c) determine, among themselves, a unique sequencing of the instructions, and
   d) generate a solution after a finite number of instructions.
4. The solution is general in the sense that it solves a whole class of problems.

Consulting such a characterization is not particularly helpful in finding a sorting algorithm. Instead, let us consider the list of names below and describe one such procedure. The procedure is sometimes called a "bubble sort": items in the list "bubble" upwards (or downwards, depending on perspective) as they are sorted to their appropriate places. The algorithm is neither an elegant nor an optimal solution, but it does work.

The bubble sort procedure starts at the top of the list and works to the bottom, comparing the names in pairs. If a pair of names is in proper order, nothing is

Anzis
Emily
Abel
Dale
Beth

done; if it is not, the members of the pair are interchanged. This is not the way that most people alphabetize a list of names, but once the algorithmic description is understood, it is seen that it does formulate how someone *could* alphabetize this list, and, in fact, any similar list, in a mechanical fashion.

Beginning with the first name, "Anzis" is compared with "Emily": since the first letter of "Anzis" is an "A" and the first letter of "Emily" is an "E," the two are in alphabetical order. The two names are not interchanged in the list. The next pair of names—"Emily" and "Abel"—is then compared. The first letters of these names are out of alphabetical order so the names are switched in the list.

In the new list, the next pair of names—"Emily" and "Dale"—is then considered. The first letters are not in proper order, so the names are interchanged.

The same comparison is made for "Emily" and "Beth," and another switch is made.

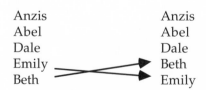

The end of the list has been reached; there is nothing more to compare. A new list has been produced from the original one:

> Anzis
> Abel
> Dale
> Beth
> Emily

During this process, three switches have been made. Whether the new list is an improvement over the old one is not really the question; the essential question is whether this procedure will, and will always, produce a correctly alphabetized list.

The bubble sort continues by starting again from the top of the new list and repeating the same actions as before. The first comparison is between "Anzis" and "Abel." Since both start with the letter "A," the second letters of the names must be examined. These are not in alphabetical order, and the two names are interchanged in the list.

"Anzis" and "Dale" are in the correct order, but not so "Dale" and "Beth." The names are switched.

The next comparison is between "Dale" and "Emily," and they are in the proper order. The end of the list has been reached, and two interchanges of names have been made. The list now looks as follows, and the procedure is repeated once more.

Abel
Anzis
Beth
Dale
Emily

"Abel" and "Anzis" are okay; so are "Anzis" and "Beth"; similarly, "Beth" and "Dale," and so, too, "Dale" and "Emily." We have reached the bottom of the list; we have made no switches; therefore, the list must be in alphabetical order. It is! But, more important, we begin to see how the procedure works and that it will work for any such list of names. It is an algorithmic solution to the alphabetization of a list of names.

This example gives an idea of what is meant by an "algorithmic" or "mechanical process." The bubble sort describes a methodic procedure through which a machine could alphabetize lists of names. It informally describes the workings of a "machine" that could do such a task, although not the machine itself. The description is clarified through a sketch of just such a "machine."

Consider a row of open boxes, placed on a table, where the box on the far left is considered the first box, the one on its right is the second box, etc.

| L___| L___| L___| .   .   .   L___|

Box 1   Box 2   Box 3   Box N

Strips of paper are ruled in the following fashion; names are written on them; and the symbol # is used to indicate the end of the name.

| A | n | z | i | s | # | | |

The strips of paper are then placed in the boxes in any order that we wish.

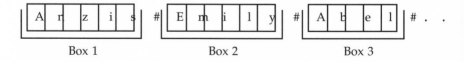

Box 1   Box 2   Box 3

Although an elaborate physical apparatus could be constructed, let us speak instead of picking up the pieces of paper from the boxes. A look-up table (like an addition or multiplication table) is also needed in which the letters of the alphabet have been placed in order as follows:

A	1
B	2
C	3
D	4
E	5
F	6

The bubble sort describes the following procedure: Take the slips of paper out of the first two boxes. find the first letters of both names in the table.

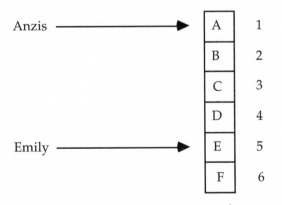

If the order of the letters in the table (1 is less than 5) corresponds to the order of the boxes, do not switch the pieces of paper between the boxes. If the order of letters is different ("Emily" and "Abel," for example), interchange the pieces of paper.

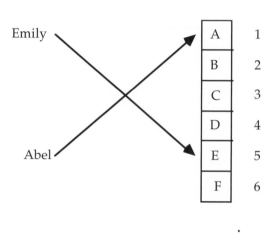

If the two letters are the same, examine the second letter on each piece of paper. Continue going through the boxes in this manner, repeatedly from start to finish, until a complete run of the boxes has been made in which no pieces of paper have been switched. The names in the boxes will then be alphabetized in the order of box 1 to the last box.

Thus, a "machine" has been described on which the bubble sort procedure could be realized as a mechanical process. The machine illustrates the generality of that procedure, but also the machine-specific limitations. Given any list of names (restricted by the number of boxes, the size of the paper strips, and the exact specification of the instructions), the same procedure, requiring no "thinking," will work.

A question arises from such demonstrations, providing one of the origins of the modern computer: Is it possible to build a physical machine on which all algorithmic processes can be realized? With the construction of such a machine, an algorithm could be defined as any procedure that can be followed by that particular machine. The same question can be raised in a different manner: How can algorithms be characterized so that we can see whether such a machine is possible? The definition with which this section began represents, informally, one such attempt to formalize the notion of an algorithm.

1. An algorithm solves a problem.
2. It solves the problem by giving a list of instructions for that problem's solution.
3. The instructions
   a) are finite in number,
   b) are unambiguous as to the actions that they describe,
   c) determine, among themselves, a unique sequencing of the instructions, and
   d) generate a solution after a finite number of instructions.
4. The solution is general in the sense that it solves a whole class of problems.

Although the bubble sort has not been explicated in minute detail, a practical understanding of it reveals all the properties of an "algorithm": The bubble sort can be described through a finite list of explicit, unambiguous instructions. When these instructions are followed, the alphabetization problem is solved. Although a different list of names might generate a different order for implementing the instructions, the sequencing of the instructions is unique for any given list of names. The solution is reached after a finite number of instructions. The bubble sort applies to a whole class of lists to be alphabetized.

Oddly, the achievement of a particular algorithm is that it reveals the type of "object" that the definition tries to formalize, not the other way around. Rather than the definition making sense of the bubble sort, the bubble sort makes sense of the definition. The practical algorithm exhibits the generality and algorithmic character of its procedure, and it does so through and as the solution of a particular problem, solved in a particular way. It is a specific algorithm, emerging from, and addressing, a specific problem.

A specific algorithm exhibits its algorithmic character rather than its being an algorithm because of its abstract properties. Until an algorithm is found, the mechanical nature of a process cannot be determined; once the algorithm is found, its idiosyncratic achievement is that it is, in its particularity, an algorithm. This is the practical accomplishment of the practical algorithm. This, in fact, is the bane of practical programming: once the adequacy of a program is seen, it is always a puzzle why it does not run.

Working through the steps of the bubble sort reveals the algorithmic character of its procedure, and this exhibited, mechanical procedure is the bubble sort's own, specific achievement. Similarly, the poetic object is a poetic object because of its own, idiosyncratic achievement. That it is a poetic object is its achievement, and its achievement, as a cultural object, is that it is a poetic object.

III

Let us return to the beginning section of the second stanza of *The Waste Land* in order to examine it as a poetic object.

Written in the style of the early prophets, the stanza begins with three concrete images that offer a characterization of the listener's life, all embedded within a question (lines 19–20). Roots are clutching at the listener; branches are growing out of "this stony rubbish" that he[2] and we know as our common world. The lines invite the listener to find their metaphorical character; they do not say what the images refer to exactly, nor is the definiteness of their referents the point of their introduction. The metaphors involve a kind of trick, asking the listener to see his life in a certain way and then asking him why, in fact, he sees life that way. The evangelist preacher is before us, challenging, threatening, almost taunting us with his or her question.

A specific answer to the question trivializes the question; nor does the speaker wish to give an answer. The question is asked rhetorically, as an opening to tell a "Son of man" not only what he does not know but what a "Son of man" cannot even guess:

> What are the roots that clutch, what branches grow
> Out of this stony rubbish? Son of man,
> You cannot say, or guess, for you know only
> A heap of broken images, where the sun beats,
> And the dead tree gives no shelter, the cricket no relief,
> And the dry stone no sound of water. Only

Literally, "Son of man" says that the listener is of humankind, a descendant of "man." The speaker invites the listener to see himself in terms of his generality: the listener, as one of many sons of man, cannot answer the question because of the desolate landscape sons of man know as their world. The commas surrounding "or guess" are important: not only can a "Son of man" not say, but—pause—an addition, an elaboration, a further reflection, hammering home the point—he cannot even make a guess, such is the state of his knowledge. Each image is specific and concrete. Together, like the opening question, they offer a characterization of the present civilization, or culture, or world of the listener; implicitly, the images ask the listener to see that they are, in fact, his world. The prophetic character of the voice has been maintained; the speaker is telling the listener what the listener himself knows of the world.

Now, the sign of hope: "Only." It is tagged on at the end of the line as if a reflection. All this is true—a land of broken images—". . . Only / . . ." Only what? This is the prophetic invitation to the listener to consider that there may be something else to be said. Only there is some shade in this sun-beaten desert (line 25) into which the listener is invited (line 26). The listener is enticed into a shadow to see what the prophet wishes to reveal, the mystery of this arid wasteland.

An argument has been made: this is the question that you—in your generality as a son of man—cannot answer or even guess at an answer for; this is the reason, what you know of the world is only this; but here, in this shadow, is the deeper mystery that awaits.

Salvation is not the theme. What is revealed is that which the listener—the one who sees the world in this way—most deeply fears. The next four lines are the only complication for reading *simpliciter.* The image Eliot creates (lines 27–29) is similar to the question of the Sphinx where the times of day serve as an analogy for the stages of a person's life, morning progressing to evening as youth turns to old age. Eliot's actual image is striking. Like all the other preceding descriptions, it is a metaphoric one. Unlike the preceding descriptions, however, this one is followed by an "answer":

I will show you fear in a handful of dust.

The reader must put together the images to see what is being said. The worst fear is not death, following in early age or looming ahead as one grows older. The greatest fear is that there is no deeper meaning to the world that we know, only that we return to the dust from which we came.

This section of the text reveals one coherent voice; that is part of its achievement. The lines belong to a prophet of the wasteland whose message is what the people most fear to hear, that this life and this wasteland are all that there is.

Once this reading of the text has been found, none of the above really needs to be said. That is the point of saying it. The analysis simply leads to and illuminates the natural analyzability of reading this particular text. It recovers the literalness of the text in the sense that, from within the laic skills of reading, this is the reading that the text itself describes. There is nothing particularly hidden, no lurking mystery, nothing absent. But therein lies its significance.

Our previous discussion of computer programming might be summarized in the following way: There are practical, laic skills of knowing how to program a computer and of knowing how a computer, in terms of programming, works. To the novice programmer, these may hardly seem to be laic skills, but they are for competent programmers, particularly when compared to the theoretical analyses of those skills that are found in mathematical logic and advanced computer science. Let us represent these laic skills as an amorphous cloud.

The Laic Skills of Programming

In writing an actual algorithm or "program," the programmer organizes these laic skills of programming; a "bubble sort" program organizes the skills of programming as a "bubble sort" procedure (figure 38).

The Laic Skills of Programming

the programmer and programming ⟶ bubble sort

Although more efficient methods than the bubble sort for sorting lists of names are available, and although the particular algorithm might be improved, for example, with a different representation of a "list" (itself an "order term" for certain programming practices), the achievement of the program—however the algorithm is written—is that it is an algorithm, that it does what it does correctly in an exhibited, mechanical fashion.

The laic skills of reading can be represented in a manner similar to the skills of programming.

The Laic Skills of Reading

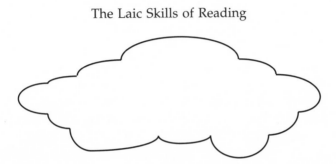

The primary achievement of a poetic object is that it finds and puts together the words so that they say exactly what they say. A poetic object describes an organization of the work of reading such that it can be read in just the manner that it is. The beauty and artistry of its lines is its literal achievement.

The Laic Skills of Reading

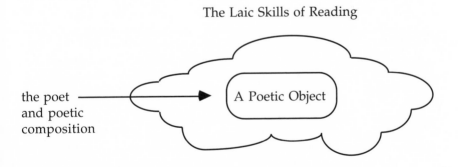

the poet and poetic composition → A Poetic Object

After the bubble sort has been discovered, it can be examined as a completed object and discussed in terms of its abstract properties as a member of the class of algorithms. Once the poetic object has been found, it can be discussed as a completed object, its imagery can be analyzed, its "intertextuality" can be examined, and a scheme of references can be worked out for its textual details. Yet its original achievement is its embodiment of poetic craft; it gets the words to say what they say in the way that they say them.

IV

A mathematical logician might tell us that our analysis of algorithms is misinformed. Similarly, a literary critic might say that our reading of this section of *The Waste Land* is misguided, or that it is only one of many possible readings, or that the intentions of the analysis are a misrepresentation of the problems of reading and are clearly wrong. A "literal" reading of the text has been presented, and the claim made that the achievement of the text is that it says what it says and that its intimate details are organized so as to say precisely that. Is anything so transparent? Is not our reading simply another instance of critical analysis?

From one perspective, the following analysis by Brooker and Bentley makes a mystery of reading the text, is purposefully flat, skews the laic skills of reading, and, in doing these things, lays the grounds for an instructed reading which builds on the summary of reading that it provides. From Brooker and Bentley's perspective, however, might not our reading be seen as purposefully twisting the text and not as a "literal" reading at all?

> This episode begins by posing two seemingly profound questions, and then by addressing the "son of man" and saying that he has no hope of answering them. The reason for his helplessness is that his experience is limited to a realm of broken images where he can see only his own shadow, where deadly heat and barren dryness keep him from knowing or guessing the answer to the original questions, where the light is so blinding and debilitating that he cannot even imagine answers. The speaker informs the son of man that relief from the heat is available under the shadow of a red rock and invites him to come into this shelter. If the son of man is willing to shift his viewpoint to the realm of shadow cast by the red rock, he will be able to see something different from his own shadows; he will see fear in a handful of dust.[3]

The claim has been made that our reading considers the text in its intimate details. Have we not, actually, avoided those details? What are the "roots that clutch" and the "branches that grow"?

The allusions are at once apparent. What indeed is the root that clutches and the branch that grows from stony rubbish but the Servant of God described by Deutero-Isaiah:

> For he grew up before him like a young plant,
> and like a root out of dry ground. . . . (Is. 53:2)[4]

The reading of the text has been slightly twisted to make a point, for the text does not say "the root" and "the branch" but "roots" and "branches." Still, the analysis offers something that the earlier one did not. And have we not missed the meaning of the "red rock"?

> Similarly with the "red rock." ("Come in under the shadow of this red rock"). In the same context with the "handful of dust," it recalls the lines from Isaiah:
>
> > Enter into the rock,
> >   and hide in the dust
> > from before the terror of the Lord. . . . (Is. 2:10)
>
> Yet what rock will hide men in safety, unless the Lord himself, who is "a shelter from the storm and a shade from the heat" (Is. 25:4); "an everlasting rock" (Is. 26:4); "the Rock of your refuge" (Is. 17:10)?[5]

Or is the rock "a biblical and Christian symbol of the church" and the red rock "a Frazerian symbol of the place of bloody sacrifice"?[6] These quotes seem to address the material detail of the text, whereas our reading glosses over them.

Eliot found the color red because he needed an extra beat in the line, because the color red distinguishes this particular rock from the others in a barren, heat-drenched landscape, because it points to a particular rock—this red rock—and because, given the ensuing context, it has some association with blood and death. By finding the color red, Eliot found these things about its use in the line. And in such a landscape, what else besides a rock would promise shade and, therein, relief?

Stated thus, such reasoning reflects a superior attitude. Do we know what Eliot was trying to do and the problems of poetic composition that he faced? What is the authority for such claims? Do they not pale in the face of the technical examination of the lines themselves?

These questions are not rhetorical; from the perspective of literary criticism, the above claims express ignorance. Whether Eliot is a master poet (or what, to different people, that might mean), he is treated as a master poet by the critical community. He wrote literary criticism himself. As a master poet and critic, he would have chosen his words for their technical resonances. Our reading omits them completely. Moreover, these lines are a reworking of lines that Eliot had written much earlier, as part of a different poem. *The Waste Land* might be seen as a pastiche, and, therein, have we not missed an essential aspect of the composition of the poem?

Consider, further, that our reading misses the possible importance of references that Eliot gives to Ezekiel, *From Ritual to Romance,* and *The Golden Bough* in the notes that he appended to the poem. There are other references as well, which might be reflected in the text.

> The only temporary refuge from the parching sun is a red rock, which emotionally recalls the Grail (sometimes figured as a stone) and Chrétien's castle of ladies, "la roche de Sanguin." It is an obscure symbol—altar-like and sacrificial, the rock of St. Peter, the grotto of the sibyl—which the protagonist remembers as the scene of his failure in the Grail quest, as the entrance way to an intense revelation of death:

> > [And I will show you] something different from either
> > Your shadow at morning striding behind you
> > Or your shadow at evening rising to meet you[;]

> The mystery is "fear in a handful of dust." Man who "fleeth as it were a shadow, and never continueth in one stay" confronts the nature of his fall. There are echoes here of "The Death of Saint Narcissus," where the glow of firelight turns a gray rock red and where the poet "shows" the dead Narcissus; and of Donne's "A Lecture upon the Shadow," or of Beaumont and fletcher's *Philaster* (Act III, scene 2), where Philaster hurls at Arethusa his angry complaint against woman:

> > . . . how that foolish man,
> > That reads the story of a woman's face
> > And dies believing it, is lost for ever;
> > How all the good you have is but a shadow,
> > I' the morning with you, and at night behind you
> > Past and forgotten. . . .

> In some tangential way the symbol of the shadow relates to sex and to the woman with whom the quester fails.[7]

In terms of larger structure, our reading avoids the problematic character of reading *The Waste Land* that the critical literature, through its numerous readings of the poem, has demonstrated. What is the thematic unity of the poem, who are the people behind the voices in the text, how does the text comment on poetry and on English prosody, what is its depiction of the then current civilization or culture? Are not these questions bound up with the reading of the poem's second stanza? Our reading exhibits a misunderstand-

ing of the nature of poetry, an ignorance of the concerns of the critical literature, and a naiveté toward the relevance of those concerns for reading *The
Waste Land* really. The reading, at best, is only the beginning of a critical
analysis, and certainly not to be raised to the achievement and aim of poetic
composition.

V

When both sides of the argument are presented, a phenomenon that stands
above the particulars of the discussion becomes apparent. The "correctness"
of our reading is only a claim about how this passage can be read; the
availability of that reading, however, illuminates the situation of professional, critical reading.

Previously, the achievement of a poetic object was depicted as follows:

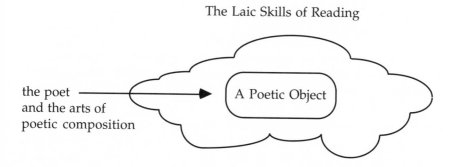

Let us place the literary critic within this picture and add as well the arts of
professional reading.

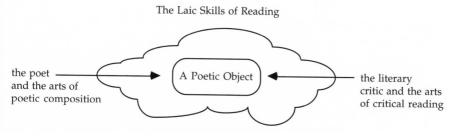

Rather than having correct and incorrect approaches to reading, there are two communities with different, if overlapping, technologies of studying and investigating the work of reading.[8]

The Arts of Professional, Critical Reading

The Laic Skills of Reading

the poet ⟶   A Poetic Object ⟵ the literary critic

The Arts of Poetic Composition

Both the poetic and the critical communities are directed to the discovery of the properties of reading-really—one through poetic composition, the other through critical analysis. By making the "text-as-such" and "reading-as-such" the loci of serious interest, both communities seem to be speaking about the same things— literal readings, allusions, prosodic structure, theme, realism, rhetorical figures, style, historical development, symbolism, the effects of a community, inter-textuality, the arts of poetic composition and analysis. Yet the substantive concerns of each community are different. The interests in reading in these communities are based on two competing technologies for the study of reading's work; the members of each community talk through each other as members of two different cultures. The text-as-such is a relic of reading, an artifact of reading's work. This fictionally objective and independent artifact stands between two cultures as the critics' totem that all talk about reading—by lay readers, by poets, and by literary critics—is about one and the same object.

For the poet, the achievement of the line

The loss of money is bewept with genuine tears.

is the line

The loss of money is bewept with genuine tears.

Words are combined and shaped to say what they say in the manner in which they say it. Similarly, the achievement of the poetic object

> Fortunatus the portrait-painter got twenty sons
> But never one likeness.[9]

is the poetic object

> Fortunatus the portrait-painter got twenty sons
> But never one likeness.

These are achievements within and as the work of reading *simpliciter:* words are put together to say what, therein, they are discovered to be read as saying. Through the work of poetic composition, the poet discovers a unique, idiosyncratic pairing of reading account ("text") and the work of reading as a poetic object. The poetic object is a discovery concerning the laic skills of reading *simpliciter.*

VI

The arts of poetic composition are the arts of an alchemy of reading. So too, however, within the community of literary critics, are instructed readings alchemies of reading practice. The technologies of reading from within which instructed readings arise are the indigenous technologies of this community's culture of reading.

Let us consider, for the last time, the first seven lines of *The Waste Land.* That the lines have much, directly, to say about the seasons or seasonal change can be doubted. The descriptions of April and winter reveal the personality of the speaker of the lines, someone who sees lilacs as breeding, memory and desire as dull roots, snow as forgetful, and someone who emphasizes the deadness of the land. They are also used as a device through which the poet moves the speaker, in memory, back through time, to contrasting periods and memories where again the seasons are used to a purpose. Rather than simple devices, the elements of the text form a whole which describes the achievement of how the lines are to be read. Once again, these lines begin:

> April is the cruellest month, breeding
> Lilacs out of the dead land, mixing
> Memory and desire, stirring
> Dull roots with spring rain.

One of the problems for literary critics has been determining the thematic unity of *The Waste Land*, if it has such a unity. The introduction to the notes which Eliot appended to *The Waste Land* contain references to Weston's *From Ritual to Romance*, Frazer's *The Golden Bough*, particularly *Adonis, Attis, Osiris* and to vegetation ceremonies.[10] By emphasizing the opening lines of the poem as a description of the seasons and seasonal change, one might read the stanza as an announcement of the major themes of the poem. The following instructed reading, part of a study of the impact of *The Golden Bough* on modern poetry, indicates how this might be done.

> By these allusions implicit in April's cruelty, Eliot links Christ and Adonis to suggest that both their deaths were part of those ritual celebrations that protected man from the overwhelming power of evil. And since Adonis was a vegetative deity it is inevitable that his departure should be matched by a "dead land" filled only with "dull roots" and "dried tubers."
>   . . .
> The "dull roots" are a vegetative analogue to human history and myth; both stretch back into "the abysm of time" which Eliot found illuminated by *The Golden Bough*. The ironic human equivalent to the "little life" of "dull roots" and "dried tubers" is found in the line: "I read, much of the night, and go south in the winter." Going south in the winter is an unconscious mimicry of the death and disappearance of the god. It is the physical, not the symbolic and spiritual, warmth of spring and summer that is sought. At the same time this endeavor to maintain perpetually the season of life and growth constitutes an implicit denial of the cyclic order of existence.[11]

The relevance of seasonal changes also emerges when Eliot's opening lines are juxtaposed with those of the Prologue of *The Canterbury Tales*.

> WHAN that Aprill with his shoures soote
> The droghte of March hath perced to the roote
> And bathed every veyne in swich licour
> Of which vertu engendred is the flour,
>   . . .
> Thanne longen folk to goon on pilgrimages

> [When April's sweet showers pierce the drought of March to the root, bathing every vein in such liqueur whose virtue it is that it engenders the flower . . . then folk long to go on pilgrimages][12]

Through this juxtaposition, Eliot's description of April seems to jumble up that of Chaucer. Chaucer celebrates the coming of spring, whereas Eliot's speaker rues spring's arrival using the same features of April that Chaucer praises. The comparison heightens the unusual sentiments toward April and winter expressed in Eliot's lines, and makes Chaucer's lines specifically relevant to those of Eliot.

This leads, perhaps, to the following instructed reading:

> Nature awakens to new life and fertility in its eternal cycle; the "shoures swete" hailed by Chaucer have come. But there is no glad welcome to this spring. The poet's feeling towards both winter and April, towards the suspension of life in which he is living, and towards a rebirth, is ambivalent, "mixing memory and desire."[13]

Here again, we see that the reading of the lines has been shifted to specifically comment on the seasons and their deeper meaning. We see as well that the recontextualization of the extracted quote has changed one of the cruel features of April—that it mixes "Memory and desire"—into an ambivalence on the part of "the poet."

As a final example, Calvin Bedient, again using the comparison with *The Canterbury Tales*, notes that there is something paradoxical in the opening of *The Waste Land*.

> Paradox and *non sequitur* between them divide up the opening block, the first saying [in the first seven lines of the block] that "happiness" (the low dream) is misery; the second, that a secular existence does not add up. Under the aegis of the first, the lively *incipit* of Chaucer's *Canterbury Tales* (virtually the *incipit* of English poetry) is turned on its head in "April is the cruellest month." To rhyme "April" with "cruel"! April breeds lilacs out of the "dead land"? Isn't that a black magic? "Winter kept us warm"? Here logic grimaces. There is logical chagrin, too, in the fancy of feeding a little life with dried tubers. This approaches conundrum, a mad science. In all, a topsy-turviness.[14]

Do the opening lines express a paradox? Sentiments which seem paradoxical, if explained, cease to remain paradoxes. Eliot's opening lines elaborate the cruelness of April: it causes the breeding of lilacs, the mixing of memory and desire, and the stirring of dull roots. Similarly, the warmth of winter (see lines 5–7 following those quoted above) is explained as the desirability of forgetting and of just keeping alive.

Because April's cruelness and winter's warmth have been explained, Bedient must skew the reading of the text to find illogic and paradox within the text's details. Eliot's text is summarized to say what it clearly does not say—that happiness is misery—and the comparison with Chaucer serves as part of this twisting of reading's ordinary work.

Each of these instructed readings relies on the skills of ordinary reading. Each attempts to show, if implicitly through its explanations, that the problems that it addresses arise from within the reading of the text. Between and among these readings, a situation of reading is generated that belongs to the critical community, not to reading *simpliciter*. The problems that emerge are problems of and for the critical community: if the Prologue of *The Canterbury Tales* is relevant to the reading of the opening lines of *The Waste Land*, what exactly is that relevance, and how is that relevance embedded in the reading of Eliot's poem?

Bedient brings to bear the full technical apparatus of literary criticism in order to solve this problem. Continuing the above quotation (with the last sentence repeated), he writes:

> In all, a topsy-turviness. Even English prosody is queered as the first three lines fall a syllable short of iambic pentameter, in a resistant way, and the fourth—with its stubborn pull and push of monosyllables, "Dull roots with spring rain"—seems intractably to stop at the halfway point of a decasyllabic. The accentual tug and clot of "Dull roots" tries to hold its own against the resonant drumming of "spring rain," with only the filmy, flimsy "with" to stand in between. Deceptive Chaucerian beauty of measure is flouted, no line is an "expected" English line, love itself is not what the "dark shimmer of sex" portends.[15]

Bedient's argument is that Chaucer's lines are written in iambic pentameter; Eliot's lines are almost iambic pentameter; as Eliot mixes up other elements of Chaucer, so he purposefully manipulates Chaucer's prosody.

In terms of argumentation, Bedient's reasoning is not particularly good. *The Canterbury Tales* might be said to define iambic pentameter for English prosody, yet Chaucer's verse—and the opening of the Prologue in particular—is not strict. If sense is to be made of Bedient's scansion, he means "trochaic" rather than "iambic pentameter," and the confusion in the description trades on a confusion within the critical literature: occasionally, any meter written with regular, two-syllable feet is described as iambic. All these things have been confounded to provide evidence for what Bedient claims.

This is not what Bedient intends; it is not a serious reading of him, and it is not what the critical enterprise concerns. Instead, using the scansion below, particularly emphasizing the second stress in the third line, the lines can be read in an awkward sing-song way in which the caesura in the first three lines can be heard as a faltering of the regularity of the meter, which then completely falls apart in the fourth line.

Áp ril | ís the | crúel lest | mónth, | bréed ing

Lí lacs | óut of | thé dead | lánd, | míx ing

Mém or | ý and | dé si | ré, | stír ring

Dúll roóts | with spríng raín.

Voiced in this way, the instructed irregularity of Eliot's cadence is a marked contrast with the heard, regular rhythms of Chaucer's verse. When this voicing is combined with the noted mixing of Chaucer's imagery in Eliot's opening lines, the reader begins to find material evidence of the presence of Chaucer in those opening lines. But who brought up Chaucer in the first place? The instructed reading is not simply an instructed reading, but it is an instructed reading for the literary community and addresses issues relevant specifically to that community.

As we have seen before, there is always "more" to Bedient than first meets the eye. His reading is directed to other aspects of the situation of professional inquiry: he is at pains to show that the first seven lines of *The Waste Land* constitute a distinct, separate "voice."[16] If the first seven lines consist of paradoxes, the remaining lines are characterized by a different figure of speech—*non sequiturs.* But there is a much more intricate way in which Bedient's reading is tied up with the arts of reading *cultura.*

When the opening of *The Waste Land* is juxtaposed with that of *The Canterbury Tales,* the similarity of the lines is not apparent; instead, what appears is a similarity in difference. Eliot can be seen to jumble up Chaucer's description; the same elements are there—April rain, rain-stirred roots, germinating plants, the passing of winter—but they are used and described in a completely different way. Similarly, Bedient's voicing of the lines is used to show that it is different from Chaucer's. Eliot's prosody is similar to Chaucer's prosody, but not the same. Therein, Bedient asks us to read that difference as the difference that Eliot intended. Eliot is seen to be purposefully "queering" English prosody and, by doing so, commenting on it. The presence of Chaucer within the lines is not ensured within reading *simpliciter;* the specific relevance of the comparison is an issue for the critical community. Bedient offers the problematic presence of Chaucer as an intrinsic feature of reading Eliot's text, the text coming to evince Eliot's own intention to make the relationship between his opening lines and Chaucer, and English prosody in general, problematic. Bedient's reading comments on the situation of professional inquiry into the reading of that text. It does so not through reasoned argumentation, but by embedding that commentary within an instructed reading—that is, within reading itself.

The annotated text in Bedient's reading is turned back on itself; the situation of inquiry is placed within the reading of the text as that which Eliot himself is commenting on. As with all the other instructed readings, but more dramatically here, critical reading folds back within itself. The distortion of the laic skills of reading becomes an alchemy of reading, but not a simple alchemy of those laic skills. It is an alchemy of the critical community's own practices of reading. Each instructed reading puts together the community's arts of reading to reveal, as a discovery about those arts, how those arts can be organized as a novel, distinctive, and original instructed reading.

12.

THE TECHNOLOGIES
AND POLITICS OF READING

The politics of the literary community concern the practices of reading. They are serious politics, for the issue of reading involves the real world—it concerns reading-really and how reading-really can and should be done. Once separated from such worldly interests, the politics of a discipline become a struggle only for recognition and authority, power, and control.

The politics of reading offer an anthropological puzzle. Knowledge of reading-really is cultural knowledge of how the community reads; the grounds of the politics of reading are deeply embedded in the practices of the critical community. What does that knowledge look like to the community, how is it articulated, and how is it tied to disciplinary politics? Such questions are central concerns of any anthropology, for they ask who is to speak authoritatively about the tribe—about its knowledge, its members' practices, and the worldliness of its projects.

I

How can or should *The Waste Land* be read, or a Shakespearean sonnet, or romantic poetry? What are the arts of reading, and how are they best described and analyzed? Anthropological investigation adds a qualifying phrase to each of these questions. What are the technologies of reading *in the critical community?* What makes a method of reading recognizably proper *for that community?* How are the structures of reading described and analyzed *by that community?* The anthropological project attempts to recover and restore the vitality of these questions in and as the life of the community.

When members of the critical community analyze the arts of reading, they understand that they are analyzing the arts of reading-really. It is reading-really for the community, and the communal practices of reading make it so, evidently. Yet, from the anthropological perspective, literary critics examine the arts of reading through a cultural prism: in analyzing reading, the critical community is already unavoidably engaged in the analysis of its own practices. The grounds, the depth, and the practicality of the community's articulations of reading's work lie within the practices of the community of which such articulations speak and to which they inescapably refer.

The figure below indicates different spheres of reading.[1] The terms "poetic influence," "intertextuality," and "misprision" (the willful misreading of a text for an intended purpose) have been included within it. Each of the terms is a reference both to the arts of poetic composition and to those of professional, critical reading.

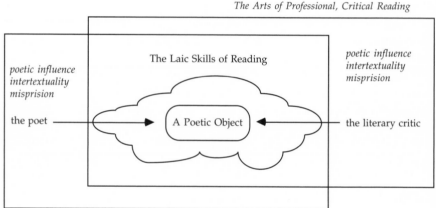

From within the sphere of poetic composition, terms such as "poetic influence," "intertextuality," and "misprision" describe aspects of poetic composition. Discovered as a novel [text/reading] pair, each poetic object recreates, sustains, modifies, and shapes the background of other such objects against which and among which it is a distinctive and original achievement. The poetic object involves an essential misprision of reading in order to create a precision of reading: its text describes a discovered, original way of reading that selfsame text; this achievement requires a reshaping of the communal arts of reading on which that achievement simultaneously depends; in this way, the poetic object has its origins in the willful recreation of the potentialities of reading. The poetic object shows the influence of other poetic objects;

it is one object among others—the reflection of, and embedded within, the practices of poetic composition. Its "intertextuality" is tied to its achievement, for its achievement as a poetic object belongs to the arts of poetic composition and lives within those arts.

Viewed from within the domain of reading *cultura*, the above statements are not incorrect, nor do they necessarily misrepresent the appreciation of the poetic object found within professional criticism. Instead, such statements are seen to involve the language of incantation: they speak generally of the poetic object; "poetic influence," "intertextuality," and "misprision" are being used to refer to the practices of poetic composition only in a general manner. In contrast, the aim of critical reading is to reveal the meaning of these terms within the detailed, material specificity of a particular text or texts. As used above, such terms retain their metaphoric character: they neither address the technical details of reading a specific text nor develop the substantive content of the terms themselves. What exactly are Eliot's sources for the opening of *The Waste Land*, how are they reflected in the text, and how did Eliot use those sources? How, specifically, was *The Waste Land* embedded in the then current arts of poetic composition, and how did Eliot modify and reshape those arts? From within the critical enterprise, as the aim of its project, the exact nature of such terms—what such terms mean concretely— needs to be revealed within the textual details of a poetic object.

Stated generally, nothing seems amiss with this project, yet a problem is embedded within it: the technical specificity of each such term is lodged within the critical community and is made available through the instructed readings of that community. The influence of poets on one another, their misreadings of each other's work, and the intertextuality of their texts are seen through the filter of the communal practices of critical reading. "Poetic influence," for example, refers to the ways that literary critics read texts, put together sources, and attempt to demonstrate that influence. To speak of the role of a protagonist in *The Waste Land*, the prosodic structure of the verse, the embeddedness of *The Waste Land* within and in contrast to then current literary traditions, the influence of Ezra Pound, the thematic character and substantive meaning of the lines, or Eliot's use of literary sources—in and as the concrete, material detail of reading *The Waste Land*—refers to the readings of the text that are described in the critical literature. The details of reading— and, therein, the meaning of "influence," "intertextuality," and "misprision" as they apply to any specific text—are hopelessly bound up with critical reading and the critical project.

The convoluted character of reading-really is apparent from this situation of reading. The cultural topics of critical reading such as poetic influence, intertextuality, and misprision refer much more descriptively to discoveries within the critical community about the community's own alchemy of reading practice. Instructed readings, for example, are a misprision of the laic skills of reading, and recognizably so: each instructed reading distorts the skills of reading *simpliciter*, willfully twisting reading to show how a text could be read. Similarly, the intertextuality of texts is known as and through the interrelationship of instructed readings, each exhibiting the relevance of a reading of a text to the ways in which the critical community reads, each reflecting, and embedding itself within, the professional situation of inquiry. "Poetic influence" refers most clearly to how the instructed readings of the community constitute and generate a current state of reading from within which, and against which, a new instructed reading is discovered and described. In the technical details of reading of which they speak, such terms formulate the community's own practices of reading, projected as the technologies of reading-really, seen and offered as the technologies of reading-really. The concrete substance and technical specificity of the terms for the critical community lie within reading *cultura*, not reading *simpliciter* or the arts of poetic composition.

Earlier, instructed readings were depicted through the following diagram, where the arrow indicates the horizonal projection of a [text/reading] pair as an instructed reading's exhibited achievement.

[text/reading]   ◀━━━━━━━━   [(text)'/reading]

The poetic object is not itself available from within an instructed reading, only the promise of such an object. Therein, the instructed reading might be represented better as the following:

◀━━━━━━━━   [(text)'/reading]

Instructed readings consist of an annotated text paired with the work of reading that recovers the adequacy of those annotations; the achievement of that pairing is the projected possibility of a distinctive poetic object.

This structure of instructed readings is a discovery about the communal practices of reading that belong to the critical community. Yet, from within that community, reading-really and critical reading are inseparable. In that instructed readings are the way in which poetic objects are known to the community, the discovery appears as concerning not instructed readings as such but the poetic object. The poetic object is found as an instructed reading which projects a poetic object. The critical community's discovery of a structure of its own practices of reading is seen not as a revelation about its own practices but as a discovery about the poetic object.

This projection onto the work of reading-really of the community's own alchemy of practice provides the basis, within the community, of its discoveries about reading-really. The arts of reading through which authorial intention is made accountable in literary criticism provide one illustration. Since a poetic text is known to the critical community as an annotated text, the opening of *The Waste Land*, for example, *is* an annotated text, and an instructed reading comes to illuminate Eliot's intentions in annotating his text in that way. Abstractly, the construction is neither "right" nor "wrong." However, in the specificity of an instructed reading of a particular text, the construction fundamentally refers to the cultured readings of the professional community and to the annotated texts that the community knows as its own achievements. The discovery is the deconstructed text—a text which is appreciated as an already and unavoidably annotated text because that is how the critical community knows texts, and a text which only aims at its completion as a poetic object because an instructed reading can never demonstrate anything more. The gap between intention and realization is filled by the instructed reading, understood as the reading which the author had originally intended. The deconstructed text comes to reveal the community's methods of reading as if those methods already belonged to the text as its author's construction; such methods are substantiated in the material details of a text as they are available from within reading *cultura*. The richness of this resource lies in the depth of its articulation of critical reading, found in the self-reflective character of the critic's own work.

In a similar manner, the entire resources of the critical community, its technologies of reading, and its alchemy of reading's laic work are examined and refined as the arts and problems of poetic composition. The misread text, the self-referential text, the open text, the closed text, the feminist text, the anticolonial text, the fascist text, the intertext text, the deconstructive text, the postmodern text, the pluralist text, the readerly text, the writerly text, the heterogeneous text, the erotic text are discovered as the critical community's own alchemical technologies of reading.

The great, received, disengaged structures of reading *cultura*—tragedy, comedy, satire, mimesis, allegory, irony, metaphor, rhetoric, prosody, plot, historical development, realism, romanticism, influence, innovation, imagery, literary meaning, characterization, theme—as well as the more recent additions, are animated by the practices of the instructed readings which sustain them. In the sociology textbook, photographs are pieced together and captioned to illustrate the adequacy of an analysis of abstract crowd behavior, the vitality of which is sustained through such pedagogic practices. The classical topics of reading's work,[2] both old and new, are animated and sustained through the critical community's practices of reading; the general structures of reading are illuminated by instructed readings which generate the communal knowledge of reading on which all depends.

Rather than being simple methodologies or structures of discursive argumentation, the critical community's indigenous technologies of reading constitute an alchemy of the practices of reading; the laic skills of reading *simpliciter* serve as a resource and a means of investigation for that alchemy. From within this entwining of lay and professional reading, through a host of contemporary studies, literary theory has increasingly come to focus on reading *cultura* as its own distinctive domain of phenomena. The discovered technologies of reading are discoveries of the critical community's own practices of reading; they are reflexive articulations of its own alchemy, projected as the structures of reading-really because that is what the community knows of reading. The discovery of criticism as the study of reading-really and the impetus of critical studies to uncover the indigenous technologies of reading constitute the community's own discovery about its own genetic and sustaining origins. Yet, arising from within the community's own reading practices and from within the community's understanding of its own practices, each such study of the structures of reading is hopelessly about and of those selfsame communal practices.

II

Recently, how we read, how we can read, and how we should read have been rediscovered as the central problems of literary studies. The traditional topics of reading have been opened for re-examination; the received terms of order—protagonist, plot, theme, narrative, meaning, imagery, characterization, prosody—are all to be reworked. The principal actors have now become the text, the reader, and reading itself. The text—

the linguistic text, the semiotic text, the underlying text, the intertext, the text of difference, the text of absence, the absent text—and the reader—the implied reader, the super-reader, the inscribed reader, the actual reader, the informed reader, the self-reading reader, the interpretive community as reader—have come to dominate literary theory as the discipline's discovery and interrogation of its own alchemy of reading, always and already projected as the properties of reading-really.

This situation of reading reflects the critical community's own appreciation of the politics of reading; it provides the community's autobiographical image of those politics.[3] Collections of articles, textbooks, special editions of journals, and studies of literary theory partition and analyze various "schools" of critical reading—formal, phenomenological, hermeneutic, dialectic, structuralist, reader-response, semiotic, feminist, poststructuralist, psychoanalytic, deconstructionist—detailing the development and interrelationship of these "schools" and assessing their contributions to the critical situation of inquiry into reading. Presented as different strategies of reading, such "perspectives" appear only as alternative methods of reading. In contrast, for the serious practitioner, each such "perspective" offers a technology for how reading-really is and should be done by the profession; each is sustained and motivated by what it reveals and says about reading particular texts. The serious political battles of the discipline—involving tenure, curriculum, teaching, the ability to publish, the recognition of meritorious work—are seen in terms of the adequate reading of texts and the formulation of the skills of such adequate readings.

The continual, ongoing debate about the meaning, structure, and technologies of reading, found in every work of literary criticism if only implicitly as an argument about how a particular text or texts can or should be read, constitutes the recognized politics of the critical community for that community. For the professional discipline, poststructural, anticolonial, or feminist criticism, and arguments about poststructural, anticolonial, or feminist criticism, ultimately concern the organizations of reading that such criticism and arguments seek to elucidate, not the independent propriety of a political position. Reading is the battleground and prize of literary criticism, and each of the "schools" of critical theory has its genetic origins in what it has to teach and show about the work of reading-really. The politics of the discipline are not something thrown on at the end as if extraneous to the worldly concerns of the discipline, a matter of simple preference or election, but are tied to the worldly aims of literary criticism in examining, really, the arts of reading.

III

The treatment of the sometimes overt, sometimes tacit politics of critical reading goes beyond the aims of this book. Nothing in this volume argues against specific critiques of those politics as they are voiced within the professional discipline. Once one sees how reading *simpliciter* is distorted within an instructed reading, talk about the "phallocentric" writings of the discipline or of a "will to power and knowledge" evidenced in the critical literature becomes much more concrete, in and as the arts of reading *cultura*. Nor, however, does this book argue for any such critique: in the ambivalence of reference to lay and professional reading, in the directedness of such critiques to the affairs of the profession, each remains a formulation within the culture of the affairs and practices of that culture. Instead, the material that has been presented indicates that such politics involve reading-really, both as reading-really is known to the critical community and as the community's technologies of reading constitute the discoverable content of that community's own practices of reading.

A beginning anthropology of reading has more central interests, not in these recognized politics of reading but in the hidden politicization of reading that permeates reading *cultura* and, therein, the critical project as a whole. Reading itself, as it is known from within the critical enterprise, is already and always a political activity. This is clarified by a simple proposition: A reading of a text, in itself, is never sufficient grounds for professional publication; reading-really, as it is known to the critical community, never ensures that anything in particular about a text is so.

Consider, again, the poetic fragment of Wilfred Owen.[4] Its achievement is that it says what it says; the problem for Owen was putting together words to discover what his intention in writing them was and how, by structuring the skills of reading through and as those words, the poetic object could be constructed to say just that, in just the way that it is said.

Elegy in April and September
(jabbered among the trees)

Hush, thrush!
Hush, missen-thrush, I listen . . .
I heard the flush of footsteps through the loose leaves,
And a low whistle by the water's brim.

Be still, daffodil!
And wave me not so bravely.
Your gay gold lily daunts me and deceives,
Who follow gleams more golden and more slim.

Look, brook!
O run and look, O run!
The vain reeds shook . . . Yet search till gray sea heaves,
And I will wind among these fields for him.

Gaze, daisy!
Stare up through haze and glare,
And mark the hazardous stars all dawns and eves,
For my eye withers, and his star wanes dim.

Once one turns away from this achievement to the properties of the instructed reading, once that achievement is viewed in terms of an instructed reading in which it is embedded, the poet becomes an academician, and poetic composition either is mystified or becomes a reflection of critical analysis. The instructed reading, having made reading mysterious, makes a mystery of itself, and becomes the endless object of fascination and investigation for the community to which it belongs. Within this conundrum of reading, reading is already, unavoidably, "political" action—it is a twisting of reading to the purposes of the critical enterprise.

The difficulty of strictly maintaining this position is that the reading practices of the profession and those of laic reading are completely entangled. Literary theory points in two directions—one to the practices of the discipline, the other to the laic skills of reading. The subtlety of this alchemy informs the work of the discipline: Stunning critical readings will turn away from the cogency of the revealed poetic object, and the mystery of that cogency, in favor of a disengaged, objective, linguistic theory to support those readings.[5] At the same time, theoretical reflections, the radicalization of which threatens the disciplinary basis of the community, are turned, instead, to reinstitute the propriety of an old, or to institute a new, canon of reading somewhere else—in the reader, in the text, in the psychoanalytic mind, in the society, in a mythic community that is the fictional projection of the community within the community itself.[6] This ambivalence is deeply ingrained in reading *cultura* and is itself part of its alchemy of reading.

The covert politics of reading—the essential and irremediable politicization of reading—lie in the unquestioned necessity of this alchemy, in the necessity of reading *cultura,* in the fact that the nature of professional competence itself, in essence, is not challenged, but only its particular effacements. The overt politics of reading, and the political battles surrounding it, take place within the domain of reading *cultura* and do not challenge the essential, underlying practices of the discipline—the omnipresence of annotated texts and instructed readings, and the inability to extricate such readings from the corpus of professional studies and from the reading practices from within which that corpus arises. The need for and propriety of reading *cultura* are maintained as the *sine qua non* of the critical enterprise and, hence, from within the critical community, as the condition of reading itself.

Although political action is frequently conceived in terms of overt behavior, the basis of such action is often spread throughout a community as a whole, living within the most ordinary of practices—in this case, in reading *cultura.* Most of the members of the critical community find no motives for questioning the appropriateness and, hence, the seriousness of their *own* work. Yet the transparent propriety of their own work is not a feature of their work alone; it resides in the fact that the practices of reading that underlie it consist of the ordinary work of a cultural community. The subterranean power of the critical discipline does not lie in recognized, overtly political behavior—in arguments about how a text can or should be read. Instead, the grounds and origins of the fundamental power of the discipline are diffuse, a part of the familiar world; they are located in the transparent need of reading *cultura* from within the practices of reading *cultura* itself.

The literary establishment gains its power at the level of practice, in and as the practices of reading "competently" and of teaching "competent" reading—through the practices of reading *cultura,* in the transparent need for those practices, in, as, and through the articulations of those practices independently of the particular articulations themselves. In this way, the political pillars of the critical discipline are not primarily a matter of orthodoxy and literary theory. Individuals need not be seen as acting politically in discussing the merits of a work of criticism. Instead, power is distributed as the shared knowledge of the discipline—not the knowledge of particular "facts," but the cultural knowledge of reading. It is found by members of the critical community in the exhibited inadequacies of reading *simpliciter;* it is found as well in the inadequacies of reading *cultura,* and therein it is found at the heart of each new technology of reading that is offered as a correction to its established predecessors.

Each new technology of reading reinstitutes the same covert politics of reading in and as the propriety of reading *cultura.* That reading has been

politicized prior to any overt manifestation of political reading is, again, em-
bodied in the simple formula: A reading of a text, in itself, is never sufficient
grounds for professional publication; reading-really, as it is known to the
critical community, never ensures that anything in particular is so about a text.

Versions of reading have proliferated; "text," "reader," and "reading" have
provided a new metaphysics of the critical community's own alchemy of
reading's laic practices. The overt political battles are over the annotated text
(how texts can or should be annotated), the instructed reading (how instructed
readings can or should be contructed), and the organization and thematization
of the corpus of professional studies (delimiting therein the literary canon and
the methods of its reading, always in the interests, and for the sensible, good
reasons, of the profession). They are struggles over how the discipline's stories
of reading are to be told and how the practices of reading should be taught.
They are struggles over reading *cultura*, over what constitutes professionally
competent reading. Yet, at the same time, they are all grounded in the arts of
reading *cultura* and the propriety and need for such practices.

IV

Any anthropology, by its very nature, raises the question of who is to speak
authoritatively, or insightfully, or descriptively about a culture. Among its
aims, an anthropology attempts to clarify what a community understands as
its knowledge of the world and how that knowledge is embedded within the
practices of that community. In this way, an anthropology is also, implicitly,
a critique; rather than accepting talk about the world as, simply, talk about the
world, it seeks to find the practices of members of a culture that make that talk
worldly talk.

A culture is lived through and known in and as the minute, concrete details
of the practices that make it, for its members, that culture. Against this
background of culture as practice—in the case of the critical community, of
reading *cultura*—members' knowledge of and formulations about that culture become available as articulations of, and are tied inseparably to, the lived
practices of that community. For the critical community, discoveries of reading are, inextricably, discoveries concerning how the community reads, and
theories of reading are, inextricably, theories about those practices of reading.
Yet, from within the community, they are also discoveries and theories of
reading-really. Whatever political battles rage within the community, a more
general "politicalization" of reading surrounds the discipline, demarcating

the work of its practitioners and their internal debates or, more exactly, making its members' work recognizable as the accountable work of the profession. From within the community, the accountable work of the profession constitutes the natural proprieties of any serious reading of a text. That the critical community is such a culture, and that it is a culture specifically of reading practice, is the heart of a beginning anthropology of reading. This is the anthropological "critique" of the critical enterprise.

To show the feasibility of an anthropology of reading, such a critique has been given. The grounds of that critique lie in coming to see how the critical community, in materially specific detail, actually reads. The aim and substance of this critique are strange, however. An anthropology of reading recovers and restores the authority of the critical community, and its politics, to the community itself; it attempts to rediscover the critical community as a community. By doing so—by rediscovering the worldly concerns of a culture as fundamentally referring to the practices of that culture—this same restoration of community comes to be the critique that an anthropology of reading offers.

NOTES

1. An Anthropology of Reading

1. Cleanth Brooks, "*The Waste Land:* Critique of the Myth," in Cleanth Brooks, *Modern Poetry and the Tradition* (Chapel Hill: University of North Carolina Press, 1939), p. 136.

2. Michael Riffaterre, "Generating Lautréamont's Text," in Josué V. Harari, ed., *Textual Strategies: Perspectives in Post-Structuralist Criticism* (Ithaca: Cornell University Press, 1979), p. 404.

3. Stanley E. Fish, "Interpreting the *Variorum,*" *Critical Inquiry* 2 (Spring 1976), reprinted in Jane P. Tompkins, ed., *Reader-Response Criticism: From Formalism to Post-Structuralism* (Baltimore: Johns Hopkins University Press, 1980), p. 164.

4. Brooks, "*The Waste Land:* Critique of the Myth," p. 138.

5. Ibid., pp. 138–39. The bracketed material has been added to Brooks's quotation to show the line structure of the poem. See "Gerontion" for the context and the omitted words.

6. I am indebted to Harcourt Brace and Company and Faber and Faber Ltd. for permission to quote excerpts from *The Waste Land* throughout this book.

7. Brooks, "*The Waste Land:* Critique of the Myth," pp. 139–40.

8. Calvin Bedient, *He Do the Police in Different Voices: "The Waste Land" and Its Protagonist* (Chicago: University of Chicago Press, 1986), p. 26.

9. Two points should be made: First, Bedient's actual claim is that a single protagonist voices all the lines in *The Waste Land.* This more general claim does not affect the analysis here, and throughout this book I stay on the more immediate level of reading the first stanza. Second, Bedient's analysis of particular lines or groupings of lines is diffused throughout his treatment of the first stanza. He returns to the discussion of various lines repeatedly; he is, in fact, quite lyrical in his own writing. An epitomizing summary of his characterizations is not possible. My intention, here and in other places in the book, is to examine the construction of his arguments and of his reading of the opening stanza of *The Waste Land,* not to distort Bedient's work. The reader is recommended and should consult his book *He Do the Police in Different Voices.*

10. See Bedient, *He Do the Police,* pp. 25–26.

2. Reading's Work

1. For background and discussion of such breaching experiments, see Harold Garfinkel, "A Conception of Experiments with 'Trust' as a Condition of Stable Concerted Actions," in O. J. Harvey, ed., *Motivation in Social Interaction* (New York: The Ronald Press Company, 1963), pp. 187–238, and Garfinkel, *Studies in Ethnomethodology* (Englewood Cliffs, N.J.: Prentice-Hall, 1967), particularly chap. 2, "Studies of the Routine Grounds of Everyday Activities." The word "work" is being used to stand for the detailed things that readers do when they read; it also gives stress to the fact that readers are implementing communal skills. The usage has its origins in the Harold Garfinkel studies of naturally organized ordinary activities. For the analysis that follows, I am indebted as well to the early work of Harvey Sacks as part of ethnomethodological culture; see Harvey Sacks, "On the Analyzability of Stories by

Children," in John J. Gumperz and Dell Hymes, *Directions in Sociolinguistics: The Ethnography of Communication* (New York: Holt, Rinehart and Winston, 1972), pp. 329–45. The stress on work and on natural organization, rather than on an analytic system, reflects Garfinkel's influence.

2. The sentence is from L. Frazier and K. Rayner, "Making and Correcting Errors during Sentence Comprehension: Eyemovements in the Analysis of Structurally Ambiguous Sentences," *Cognitive Psychology* 14 (1982): 178–210, cited and discussed in Robert G. Crowder, *The Psychology of Reading: An Introduction* (New York: Oxford University Press, 1982), p. 123.

3. See Crowder, *The Psychology of Reading*, p. 123, for a discussion of Frazier and Rayner's work, and Frazier and Rayner, "Making and Correcting Errors during Sentence Comprehension." In general, studies of eye movement during reading show regularity in pacing, placement of eye fixation, length of fixations, and the asymmetrical use of parafoveal vision. Since these regularities are taught and learned as the skills of reading, they indicate how close society comes to embed itself in the smallest details of our actions—in this case, in the pattern of eye movements across and down a page. As developed below, however, eye movement cannot be separated from a reader's active engagement in using a text as a description of an organization of reading's work. As experimental studies increasingly focus on natural situations of reading, greater attention and recognition may be given to this relationship.

4. The figure appears as Fig. 50 in K. Koffka, *Principles of Gestalt Psychology* (London: Routledge and Kegan Paul Ltd., 1935), p. 173, reproduced by permission of the publisher.

5. Roger Farr and Nancy Roser, *Teaching a Child to Read* (New York: Harcourt Brace Jovanovich, 1979). The examples are from pages 173, 180, and 176, respectively.

6. "The Painted House" by Margaret Early from *Going Places, Seeing People* by Elizabeth K. Cooper (New York: Harcourt Brace Jovanovich, 1974), pp. 8–9, quoted in Farr and Roser, *Teaching a Child to Read*, p. 59. Sexist aspects of the story might be excused because of the way that life sometimes is: Father is the initiator of the action, while Mother is an appreciative collaborator; Father paints sky and clouds, while Mother paints flowers; Father apparently stands, while Mother scrunches down on the ground. The references to the house overdetermine the sexism and make it apparent: for Mother, it is "an" or "the" house; for Father, it is "his house." It must be noted, however, that "sexism" here refers to a configuration of writing from a current perspective and sensitivity, not to ones necessarily present when the story was written. My comments should not be taken in any manner as reflections of or about the author, her intentions, her sensitivities, etc.

7. Crowder, *The Psychology of Reading*, p. 201.

8. Wilfred Owen, *The Collected Poems of Wilfred Owen*, edited with an Introduction and Notes by C. Day Lewis and with a Memoir by Edmund Blunden (London: Chatto and Windus, 1963), p. 142.

9. See Aron Gurwitsch, *The Field of Consciousness* (Pittsburgh: Duquesne University Press, 1964), pp. 105–23. My appreciation of Gurwitsch comes through Harold Garfinkel, who, in his lectures, developed the relevance of Gurwitsch's work for ethnomethodological studies. In the text, I use "good continuation" and "gestalt texture" to stress the dynamic, temporal, and temporally building character of reading; a completed "gestalt" is not available from within an ongoing course of reading, but is projected as a developing yet unfulfilled whole.

10. The examination of such pairings originated and developed in collaborative studies of mathematicians' work with Harold Garfinkel; his influence and general formulations of this pairing are reflected here. For early work on mathematics, see

Eric Livingston, *The Ethnomethodological Foundations of Mathematics* (London: Routledge and Kegan Paul, 1986). Eric Livingston, *Making Sense of Ethnomethodology* (London: Routledge and Kegan Paul, 1987), discusses the pair relationship for mathematics.

11. The use of gestalt analogies for describing discovered organizations of practice was developed by Garfinkel in the work surrounding Harold Garfinkel, Michael Lynch, and Eric Livingston, "The Work of a Discovering Science Construed with Materials from the Optically Discovered Pulsar," *Philosophy of the Social Sciences* 11 (1981): 131–58.

12. Juvenal, *Satires* 13.134. The translation "Lost money is bewept with genuine tears" appears in Robert Burton, *The Anatomy of Melancholy*, ed. Floyd Dell and Paul Jordan-Smith (New York: Tudor Publishing Company, 1927), p. 308. The concern here is with the line in English. No claims are made about Juvenal; the translation used in the text apparently reflects the preference in English for nominal over verbal expressions. I thank Peter Toohey for his comments and his assistance with the Latin. He cautioned me on using the translation in the text to speak of Juvenal's original writings.

3. The Exegetical Demonstration

1. This poem appears with the following note by the editor: "[The British Museum] has two drafts of this poem, one entitled *Ode to a Poet reported Missing; later reported Killed.* [Harold Owen] has one draft. I print the first four stanzas only; the remaining three are markedly inferior." Wilfred Owen, *The Collected Poems of Wilfred Owen*, edited with an Introduction and Notes by C. Day Lewis and with a Memoir by Edmund Blunden (London: Chatto and Windus, 1963), p. 142. Interest here and in chap. 12 focuses entirely on the text as it appears in this source. Whether called a "poem" or a "poetic fragment," independently of its possible "collaborative" articulation, the text, embedded in the lived work of its reading, constitutes a "poetic object." My discussion throughout this book treats it as such, and I use it here for the poem's essentially clarifying character.

2. Ethnomethodological studies of science, in general, have focused on discovery as that which sustains the sciences as practice. Here, however, the formulation of an "exegetical demonstration" was stimulated by recent work of Dusan Bjelic on Galileo's use of demonstrations. See, for example, "Equipmental Availability of Galilean Physics," working paper, University of Southern Maine, Fall 1992.

3. This passage was occasioned by a section of William Ray's *Literary Meaning: From Phenomenology to Deconstruction* (Oxford: Basil Blackwell, 1984), pp. 27–35. Following a discussion of the continual activity of a reader in concretizing the intentional text as depicted by Ingarden, while reviewing Iser's writings, Ray writes on page 35, "It is not the essential 'suspended' nature of the reading consciousness that keeps it from receding into fantasy, but rather the textual extension, that is, the constant barrage of new schema (Sartre would say pure meanings) that need to be integrated." Ray's treatment of the work of Ingarden and Iser is compatible with many of the themes in this book. The direct influences, however, were not the writings of these authors but the teachings of Harold Garfinkel on the analysis of naturally organized ordinary activities and my engagement in the close (as an anonymous reviewer described it, "microscopic") inspection of the lived work of reading.

4. The pairing of such objects as [accounts of work/associated work of the account] arose in Garfinkel's and my collaboration on mathematicians' work; his influence and formulations of this pairing are reflected here. For the ethnomethodological "bracketing" of an activity, see Harold Garfinkel and Harvey Sacks, "On Formal Structures of Practical Actions," in John C. McKinney and Edward Tiryakian, eds., *Theoretical Sociology: Perspectives and Developments* (New York: Appleton-Century-Crofts, 1970),

150 _Notes_

pp. 338–66, and as an introduction, see the discussion in Livingston, _Making Sense of Ethnomethodology_. The notation implies the relative constancy of the social phenomenon named within the brackets. This "reverse" side of the bracket notation is used here to indicate that a poetic object is an object, and that this is its achievement as an organization of the work of reading.

5. See chap. 2, n. 11.

6. "Fortunatus the R. A.," a translation by Dudley Fitts, in Dudley Fitts, _Poems from the Greek Anthology in English Paraphrase_ (New York: New Directions, 1956), p. 91. The poem is treated here as a poem in English; it is examined in terms of how it is read in English. No claims are made about the original poem or the translation of it.

7. The fact that the poem might be read differently does not influence the substance of the argument. Sometimes the fact that texts can always be read differently is used to argue for an inherent ambiguity within the activity of reading. On the one hand, such ambiguity is a reflection that reading's work is essentially practical, allowing the reader to keep reading. On the other hand, as a practical activity, reading has definiteness; it is not inundated by the possibility of variant readings. In general, only when reading is disengaged from the activity of reading itself does the work of reading not have a practically objective character.

8. Carl Fernbach-Flarsheim, "death poem #3," in Eugene Wildman, ed., _The Chicago Review Anthology of Concretism_ (Chicago: The Swallow Press, 1967), p. 83.

4. Problems of Reading

1. The term "reading _simpliciter_" has its origins in Dorion Cairns, "An Approach to Phenomenology," in _Philosophical Essays in Memory of Edmund Husserl_, ed. Marvin Farber (Cambridge: Harvard University Press, 1940), pp. 3–18, where a distinction is made between an "object _simpliciter_" and an "intentional object."

2. Dylan Thomas, _The Collected Poems of Dylan Thomas: 1934–1952_ (New York: New Directions Books, 1955), p. 81.

3. The fact that a ewe does not carry a lamb for nine months is irrelevant. The identification of a woman with her womb and the description of it as a grave (if this is the intended reading of the line) are objectionable, as is a vagina's (possible) description as a "wrinkled undertaker's van." As well, the reader should note that, in the analysis by Tindall given below, Tindall's image of a potent Dylan Thomas seems to be projected over and above even what Dylan Thomas seems to project, at least in this sonnet.

4. William York Tindall, _A Reader's Guide to Dylan Thomas_ (London: Thames and Hudson, 1962), pp. 141–42. Arabic numerals reference pages of poems in the English edition of _The Collected Poems_, published by J. M. Dent and Sons Ltd., 1952; Roman numerals refer to the number of a sonnet in the "Altarwise" collection. The reference to "the old gentleman who lost his mandrake" is to the first sonnet of the "Altarwise" series.

5. Ibid., pp. 142–43.

6. Elder Olson, _The Poetry of Dylan Thomas_ (Chicago: University of Chicago Press, 1954), p. 13.

7. Note from original source with bracketed material as given in that source: _CP_ [_The Collected Poems of Dylan Thomas_ (Norfolk, Conn.: New Directions, 1953)], p. 110.

8. Note from original source: _CP_, p. 108.

9. Note from original source: _CP_, p. 29.

5. The Naturally Analyzable Text

1. For an analysis of the opening of telephone calls as summons-answer sequences, see Emanuel A. Schegloff, "Sequencing in Conversational Openings," *American Anthropologist* 70, no. 6 (1968): 1075–95. The discussion here reflects Harold Garfinkel's treatment and analysis of such materials.

2. The investigation of the natural analyzability of naturally organized ordinary activities is due to Harold Garfinkel. Early studies in ethnomethodology may be found in Harold Garfinkel, *Studies in Ethnomethodology* (Englewood Cliffs, N.J.: Prentice-Hall, 1967). Eric Livingston, *Making Sense of Ethnomethodology* (London: Routledge and Kegan Paul, 1987), provides an introduction.

3. Even with simple sums such as 25 plus 7, practical methods are often used: 7, for example, has a 5 in it (7 = 5 + 2), so 25 plus 7 is 30 (25 + 5) with 2 left over, hence 32.

4. Nor do such machines remove the locally developing character of the practices involved in their use.

5. I am indebted to Marcia Daniels for this example.

6. I am told that in Japan, merchants, at least in the 1970s, frequently checked electronic calculations by repeating the computation with an abacus. A computer produces a result, probably correct but possibly not. Through the use of an abacus, the practices through which a calculation is actually performed are exhibited and can be inspected in the course of the calculation. I thank Rosetta Livingston for the example.

7. The problem is illustrated by an excerpt from the definition of "gargoylism" appearing in Leland E. Hinsie and Robert Jean Campbell, *Psychiatric Dictionary*, 4th ed. (New York: Oxford University Press, 1970), p. 318. In the original, the text appears as one continuous sentence; here it has been reshaped to help indicate the stress and phrasing of a possible reading.

The child resembles an achondroplastic dwarf
and shows multiple skeletal deformities
    (short neck,
    dorsal kyphosis,
    deformed thorax and long bones,
    flexion deformities of all joints,
    and maldevelopment of the skull vault and facial bones),
hideous features
    (thickened skin and soft tissues,
    large head with widely spaced eyes and flattening of the bridge of the nose,
    coarse lips,
    protruding tongue,
    stridulent mouth breathing,
    and an apathetic, bovine expression),
hepatosplenomegaly,
corneal clouding,
mental retardation (31x.2).

8. The actual quotation, translated with minor variations in the literature, reads roughly, "With my own eyes I saw the Cumaean Sibyl hanging in a jar, and when the

boys asked her, 'What do you want?' she answered, 'I want to die.'" See, for example, B. C. Southam, *A Student's Guide to the "Selected Poems" of T. S. Eliot* (New York: Harcourt, Brace and World, 1968), p. 71, and Elizabeth Drew, *T. S. Eliot: The Design of His Poetry* (New York: Charles Scribner's Sons, 1949), p. 68. Robert J. Baker confirmed the sense of the translation and, particularly, that the Sibyl is hanging in a jar. His exact translation went unrecorded.

9. There may be irony in this line as well: While the woman claims to be a "true" German, her conversational speech may not be that good. Herman Beyersdorf and Gabriele Ouellette, among other native speakers, assisted with the translation and commented on the line; responsibility for its reading, particularly in the context of the poem, is mine.

10. Cleanth Brooks, "*The Waste Land:* Critique of the Myth," in Cleanth Brooks, *Modern Poetry and the Tradition* (Chapel Hill: University of North Carolina Press, 1939), pp. 138–39.

11. Calvin Bedient, *He Do the Police in Different Voices: "The Waste Land" and Its Protagonist* (Chicago: University of Chicago Press, 1986), p. 9.

12. Drew, *T. S. Eliot: The Design of His Poetry*, p. 68.

13. John B. Vickery, *The Literary Impact of "The Golden Bough"* (Princeton: Princeton University Press, 1973), pp. 248–49.

14. Bedient, *He Do the Police*, pp. 19–20.

15. Note from the original source: Besides those already cited, valuable commentaries on the poem include R. P. Blackmur, "T. S. Eliot," *Hound and Horn*, I (March, 1928), 187–213; Wilson, Unger, pp. 177–84; Ross Williamson, *The Poetry of T. S. Eliot*, pp. 78–150; F. R. Leavis, *New Bearings in English Poetry* (London, 1932), pp. 91–114; C. R. Jury, *T. S. Eliot's The Waste Land: Some Annotations* (Adelaide, 1932); Matthiessen; Cleanth Brooks, "*The Waste Land:* Critique of the Myth," Unger, pp. 319–48; Williamson, *A Reader's Guide to T. S. Eliot*, pp. 115–54. See also H. Reid MacCallum, "*The Waste Land* after Twenty-five Years," *Hear and Now*, I (December, 1947), 16–24; Eric Mesterton, *The Waste Land: Some Commentaries* (Chicago, 1943); Derek Traversi, "*The Waste Land* Revisited," *Dublin Review*, No. 443, 1948, pp. 106–23; Drew, pp. 58–90; C. M. Bowra, *The Creative Experiment* (London, 1949), pp. 159–88.

16. Note from the original source: Cf. Philippe, *Bubu of Montparnasse*, chap. 1: "A man walks carrying with him all the properties of his life, and they churn about in his head. Something he sees awakens them, something else excites them. For our flesh has retained all our memories, and we mingle them with our desires."

17. Note from the original source: James Thomson, "To Our Ladies of Death," *The City of Dreadful Night, and Other Poems* (London, 1910), p. 148.

18. Note from the original source: Cf. Rupert Brooke, *Letters from America* (New York, 1916), p. 174; Matthiessen, pp. 92–93.

19. Grover Smith, *T. S. Eliot's Poetry and Plays: A Study in Sources and Meaning* (Chicago: University of Chicago Press, 1956), pp. 72–73.

6. Order Terms and Competent Systems

1. The use of "orderlinesses" is borrowed from Harold Garfinkel; the descriptiveness of the term for reading's work is developed in this chapter.

2. I am indebted to Michelle Arens and Roger Pitcher for their suggestions on "reading *cultura*." Reading *cultura* is "reading with culture"; it refers to the cultivated practices of reading found in the critical community and is used in contrast with the laic practices of reading *simpliciter*.

3. The discussion of psychoanalysis is intended here only to illustrate the use of order terms; it is based on preliminary research on the work of psychoanalysis, partially presented in the paper "Freud and the Structures of Intention" at the Annual Meetings of the American Sociological Association, 1990. I am indebted to Richard Rosenstein and Marcia Daniels for a number of discussions concerning this material. The central figure in the development of similar issues among psychoanalysts seems to be Merton Gill. See Merton M. Gill, *Analysis of Transference: Volume I* (New York: International Universities Press, 1982), and Merton M. Gill and Irwin Z. Hoffman, *The Analysis of Transference: Volume II* (New York: International Universities Press, 1982).

4. The example is quoted in Goold Brown, *The Grammar of English Grammars* (New York: William Wood and Company, 1882), p. 407.

5. *Julius Caesar*, III.ii, in Irving Ribner and George Lyman Kittredge, eds., *The Complete Works of Shakespeare* (Waltham: Xerox College Publishing, 1971), p. 1027.

6. The manner of expression here borrows from Dusan Bjelic. As told to me by Dusan, he would perform a Galilean demonstration with pendulums. He would then také apart the apparatus and point out that no matter how closely the weights and cords were inspected, the demonstration did not reside in them.

7. *Macbeth*, I.v, in Ribner and Kittredge, eds., *The Complete Works of Shakespeare*, p. 1297, cited as an example of irony in Joseph T. Shipley, *Dictionary of World Literature* (New York: Philosophical Library, 1953), p. 239.

8. The scansions are given and compared by Harvey Gross in *Sound and Form in Modern Poetry: A Study of Prosody from Thomas Hardy to Robert Lowell* (Ann Arbor: University of Michigan Press, 1973), pp. 38–39. The first two lines of poetry are from "Sunday Morning" by Wallace Stevens and can be found in Wallace Stevens, *The Collected Poems of Wallace Stevens* (New York: Alfred A. Knopf, 1954), p. 70. The second two are the opening lines of the second stanza of *The Waste Land*.

9. The scansions are, again, given and compared by Gross in *Sound and Form in Modern Poetry*, p. 38.

10. *Julius Caesar*, I.i, in Ribner and Kittredge, eds., *The Complete Works of Shakespeare*, p. 1010.

11. Calvin Bedient, *He Do the Police in Different Voices: "The Waste Land" and Its Protagonist* (Chicago: University of Chicago Press, 1986), p. 26.

12. Ibid., p. 22.

13. My use of the phrase "competent systems" was stimulated by Harold Garfinkel's distinguishing the conversation-analytic turn-taking mechanism from other studies of naturally organized ordinary activities as a "competent" system. (For the turn-taking mechanism, see Harvey Sacks, Emanuel Schegloff, and Gail Jefferson, "A Simplest Systematics for the Organization of Turn-Taking in Conversation," *Language* 50 [1974]: 696–735.) The idea here is that systems of order terms are intended, and serve, as competent systems for analyzing the natural organization of ordinary activities—whether the actions of participants in psychoanalytic consultation or the work of reading a text.

14. This discussion is intended only to give a sense of rhetorical analysis. See Geoffrey N. Leech, *A Linguistic Guide to English Poetry* (London and New York: Longman, 1969); Richard A. Lanham's books *Analyzing Prose* (New York: Charles Scribner's Sons, 1983) and *A Handlist of Rhetorical Terms: A Guide for Students of English Literature* (Berkeley: University of California Press, 1968); Donald Rice and Peter Schafer, *Rhetorical Poetics: Theory and Practice of Figural and Symbolic Reading in Modern French Literature* (Madison: University of Wisconsin Press, 1983); and Bernard Dupriez, *A Dictionary of Literary Devices*, translated and adapted by Albert W. Halsall (London: Harvester Wheatsheaf, 1991). The first line of Marullus's speech is discussed as a "dehumanizing" metaphor in Leech, *A Linguistic Guide*, p. 158.

15. The background for this formulation comes from two different traditions, one originating in the work of Ferdinand de Saussure and the other in the work of Talcott Parsons, to which I was introduced by Garfinkel. For Parsons, see Ian Craib, *Modern Social Theory: From Parsons to Habermas* (London: Harvester Press, 1984), and Jonathan H. Turner, *The Structure of Sociological Theory* (Homewood: The Dorsey Press, 1974). A similar relationship holds between mathematical logic and the naturally accountable work of mathematical theorem proving. See Eric Livingston, *The Ethnomethodological Foundations of Mathematics* (London: Routledge and Kegan Paul, 1986).

7. The Deeply Reasoned Text

1. Grover Smith, *T. S. Eliot's Poetry and Plays: A Study in Sources and Meaning* (Chicago: University of Chicago Press, 1956), pp. 72–74.

2. John B. Vickery, *The Literary Impact of "The Golden Bough"* (Princeton: Princeton University Press, 1973), pp. 248–49.

3. Jewel Spears Brooker and Joseph Bentley, *Reading "The Waste Land": Modernism and the Limits of Interpretation* (Amherst: University of Massachusetts Press, 1990), p. 62.

4. Richard P. Feynman, Robert B. Leighton, and Matthew Sands, *The Feynman Lectures on Physics* (Reading: Addison-Wesley Publishing Company, 1963), vol. 1, chap. 2, pp. 1–2.

5. Dudley Fitts, "Fortunatus the R. A.," in Dudley Fitts, *Poems from the Greek Anthology in English Paraphrase* (New York: New Directions, 1956), p. 91.

6. The example, though not used in the context of reading, again owes itself to Garfinkel. See chap. 2, n. 11.

7. The following discussion draws on a number of different commentaries on *The Waste Land*. In particular, I have used elements from Eric Thompson's analysis in the appendix to his book *T. S. Eliot: The Metaphysical Perspective* (Carbondale: Southern Illinois University Press, 1963), pp. 143–60. The discussion is not intended as a representation of Thompson's analysis or his method of working. Instead, the discussion is used as a heuristic introduction to the type of reading that begins to be articulated in later sections of the chapter.

8. Again, the ideas here are borrowings from Eric Thompson's analysis in the appendix to his book *T. S. Eliot: The Metaphysical Perspective*, pp. 143–60. I have not tried to represent Thompson's writings or his arguments; I have used elements in his work to build a picture of a particular way of working that is elaborated and made more realistic later in this chapter. See n. 7 above. If the voice of a single protagonist runs throughout *The Waste Land*, and one reads the opening stanzas as Cleanth Brooks does, considerations such as these may be essential to a "reading" of the poem.

9. Calvin Bedient, *He Do the Police in Different Voices: "The Waste Land" and Its Protagonist* (Chicago: University of Chicago Press, 1986), p. 26.

10. Ibid., p. 17.

11. Ibid., p. 26.

12. Ibid.

13. Ibid., pp. 26–27.

14. See ibid., p. 20.

15. See ibid., p. 20.

16. Ibid., p. 9.

17. Ibid., p. 22.

8. The Instructed Reading

1. The basic idea of the story is due to Herbert Livingston. I thank Bruce Knight for his considerations on its modification. For the analysis that follows the story and questions, one should compare Harvey Sacks, "On the Analyzability of Stories by Children," in John J. Gumperz and Dell Hymes, *Directions in Sociolinguistics: The Ethnography of Communication* (New York: Holt, Rinehart and Winston, 1972), pp. 329–45. The influence is not direct, but one of general background; I find myself doing an analysis that I think similar to the type that Sacks, in his early work, might have done. The stress on natural analyzability reflects the influence of Harold Garfinkel.

2. The photographic sequences are those of Eadweard Muybridge and can be found, for instance, as plates 23 and 105, respectively, in Eadweard Muybridge, *The Human Figure in Motion* (New York: Dover Publications, Inc., 1955). The analysis of these photographs was occasioned by a similar treatment of a sequence of photographs by Dušan Bjelić in Bjelić, "The Praxiological Validity of Natural Scientific Practices as a Criterion for Identifying Their Unique Social-Object Character: The Case of the 'Authentication' of Goethe's Morphological Theorem," *Qualitative Sociology* 15, no. 3 (1992): 221–45. The emphasis here is, first, on the detailed analysis that we do in order to see not the action but the sequence of photographs as an account of that action, and, second, on the naturalness of this analysis in the sense that the analysis is part of and inseparably tied to seeing the photographs as constituting such an account.

3. Roger Farr and Nancy L. Roser, *Placement Test for Primary Grades: Teacher's Edition* (River Forest, Ill.: Laidlaw Brothers, 1976), p. 13, reprinted in Roger Farr and Nancy Roser, *Teaching a Child to Read* (New York: Harcourt Brace Jovanovich, 1979), p. 72. A "cloze" passage is one in which, for a given number n, every nth word in a text is removed; in a "modified" cloze passage, the words have been removed selectively. In either case, such a passage depends on, and its solution exhibits, the natural analyzability of reading. Cloze passages are used as teaching devices and as tests of reading level: a third-grader, for example, should be able to determine a certain percentage of the words deleted from a text written at the third-grade level. The use of a formula for deleting words gives the appearance of an objective testing procedure; however, reading-level assessment requires a normalized background of response to the particular passage whichever procedure is used.

4. Studies of reading comprehension also transform the natural analyzability of reading into an objective account of reading, but the concern here is with literary criticism.

5. The problematic relationship discussed below between the photographs and their associated captions, as well as the pervasive presence of such illustrations in (U.S.) introductory sociology textbooks, was pointed out to me by Harold Garfinkel through some passing remarks. The analysis here and in chap. 10 undoubtedly mirrors, at least in some respects, his own.

6. Both photographs appear in John J. Macionis, *Sociology*, 2nd ed. (Englewood Cliffs, N.J.: Prentice-Hall, 1989), p. 571 and p. 508 respectively; they could not be reproduced in this book. The central phenomenon, however, is the relationship between the photographs and their captions. I felt it best to use the actual captions rather than introduce photographs and captions of my own. References are given for the other photographs below, but once the phenomenon is seen, a wide range of textbooks will provide ample illustrations.

7. The photograph appears in ibid., p. 508. The picture is not clearly that of a woman: the shoulders are quite large, the hair may be a wig, the perspective of the photograph makes it difficult to judge relative height. At first sight, the person seems to be a woman; the ensemble resembles that which a woman might wear. For clarity of expression, the feminine pronoun seemed preferable to an indefinite one.

8. The theme of which could be seen as their unthematic character.

9. Macionis, *Sociology*, 2nd ed., p. 571.

10. Ibid., p. 508.

11. Different styles of captions are found; some, for example, use "indexical expressions" such as the word "this." Thus, a photograph of a crowded public park might be captioned "This is the way many families spend leisure time together." Such a caption requires not only the active participation of the reader to find how the photograph could illustrate the caption, but a recognition of that involvement—the reader is instructed to look. Macionis, *Sociology*, 2nd ed., from which many of the examples in this book come, offers a more sophisticated and professional style. Written as independent, objective statements about the social world, the captions are actually disassociated from the photographs that illustrate them, requiring the reader to find in a photograph an illustration of the truth of its caption. The relevance of this distinction is elaborated somewhat in the beginning of chap. 10. (For indexical expressions and their bearing on sociological inquiry, see Harold Garfinkel, *Studies in Ethnomethodology* [Englewood Cliffs, N.J.: Prentice-Hall, 1967], chap. 1, and Harold Garfinkel and Harvey Sacks, "On Formal Structures of Practical Actions," in John C. McKinney and Edward Tiryakian, eds., *Theoretical Sociology: Perspectives and Developments* [New York: Appleton-Century-Crofts, 1970], pp. 338–366.)

12. John E. Farley, *Sociology*, 2nd ed. (Englewood Cliffs, N.J.: Prentice Hall, 1992), p. 228.

13. Macionis, *Sociology*, 2nd ed., p. 70.

14. Ibid., p. 184.

15. John J. Macionis, *Sociology*, 4th ed. (Englewood Cliffs, N.J.: Prentice-Hall, 1993), p. 49.

16. Calvin Bedient, *He Do the Police in Different Voices: "The Waste Land" and Its Protagonist* (Chicago: University of Chicago Press, 1986), p. 26.

17. Bedient, *He Do the Police*, p. 20.

18. Ibid., pp. 26–27.

19. Garfinkel's rendering theorem states that a social object (as a gestalt ensemble of indexical particulars) is rendered by the methods of constructive sociological analysis as a collection of signs, written as

$$[\ ] \longrightarrow (\ )$$

or, as one of Garfinkel's examples, a summoning telephone is rendered basically as a "ringing phone," a summoning-phone-prime:

[Summoning Phone] ⟶ (Summoning Phone)

Clearly, the material in the text comes from considerations involved in this theorem.

This material leads to a possible "categorical algebra." If "text" and "text-prime" are understood as artifacts of reading—as the "text" and the "annotated text" respectively—the diagram below

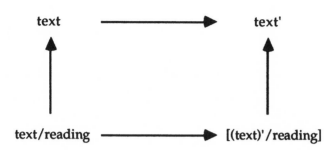

is transformed by a "reversal of arrows" into the following:

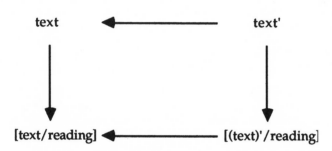

9. The Cultural Object

1. Cleanth Brooks, "*The Waste Land:* Critique of the Myth," in Cleanth Brooks, *Modern Poetry and the Tradition* (Chapel Hill: University of North Carolina Press, 1939), p. 136.

2. Note from original source: Louis Untermeyer, *Freeman*, 6 (17 January 1923); 453, rpt. in *T. S. Eliot: The Critical Heritage, vol. 1*, ed. Michael Grant (London: Routledge and Kegan Paul, 1982), 151.

3. Note from original source: *New Republic*, 33 (7 February 1923): 294–95; rpt. in *T. S. Eliot: The Critical Heritage, vol. 1*, 158, 160.

4. John T. Mayer, "*The Waste Land:* Eliot's Play of Voices," in Lois A. Cuddy and David H. Hirsch, eds., *Critical Essays on T. S. Eliot's "The Waste Land"* (Boston: G. K. Hall, 1991), p. 265.

5. Ian Hamilton, "*The Waste Land*," in Graham Martin, ed., *Eliot in Perspective: A Symposium* (London: Macmillan, 1970), p. 104.

6. Calvin Bedient, *He Do the Police in Different Voices: "The Waste Land" and Its Protagonist* (Chicago: University of Chicago Press, 1986), p. ix.

7. Note from original source: Calvin Bedient, *He Do the Police in Different Voices: "The Waste Land" and Its Protagonist* (Chicago: University of Chicago Press, 1986).

8. Jewel Spears Brooker and Joseph Bentley, *Reading "The Waste Land": Modernism and the Limits of Interpretation* (Amherst: University of Massachusetts Press, 1990), pp. 3, 6. As noted previously, Bedient's claim is that, in addition to there being four distinctive voices in the opening stanza, and multiple voices throughout *The Waste Land*, all are performances of one protagonist. This claim concerns the larger structure of *The Waste Land*.

9. For the source of the reference to a possible relationship between Freud's writings and the first stanza, see John B. Vickery, "Two Sources of 'The Burial of the Dead,'" *Literature and Psychology* 10 (Winter 1960): 3–4, reprinted in Jay Martin, ed., *A Collection of Critical Essays on "The Waste Land"* (Englewood Cliffs, N.J.: Prentice-Hall, 1968), pp. 27–28.

10. Bedient, *He Do the Police*, p. 26.

11. Brooks, "*The Waste Land*: Critique of the Myth," p. 139.

12. The following texts provide an introduction to the literature: Michael Grant, ed., *T. S. Eliot: The Critical Heritage*, vol. 1 (London: Routledge and Kegan Paul, 1982); Jay Martin, ed., *A Collection of Critical Essays on "The Waste Land"* (Englewood Cliffs, N.J.: Prentice-Hall, 1968); Robert H. Canary, *T. S. Eliot: The Poet and His Critics* (Chicago: American Library Association, 1982); Brooker and Bentley, *Reading "The Waste Land,"* pp. 3–6; and Lois A. Cuddy and David H. Hirsch, "Introduction," in Cuddy and Hirsch, eds., *Critical Essays on T. S. Eliot's "The Waste Land"* (Boston: G. K. Hall, 1991) pp. 1–24, both for the article's summary and for its extensive references.

13. The origins of my use of "situation of inquiry" are no longer clear; most likely it is Garfinkel's, and I recall his using the phrase in answer to my complaint about a different expression.

14. Brooker and Bentley, *Reading "The Waste Land,"* pp. 61–62.

15. Ibid., p. 60.

16. Ibid., p. 63.

17. Note from original source: Jewel Spears Brooker, "When Love Fails: Reading *The Waste Land* with Undergraduates," in *Approaches to Teaching Eliot*, 103–8.

18. Brooker and Bentley, *Reading "The Waste Land,"* p. 63.

19. For a study of the relationship between worksite practice and discovery in astronomy, see Harold Garfinkel, Michael Lynch, and Eric Livingston, "The Work of a Discovering Science Construed with Materials from the Optically Discovered Pulsar," *Philosophy of the Social Sciences* 11 (1981): 131–58.

10. A Family Romance

1. See chap. 8, n. 5. The example is from John J. Macionis, *Sociology*, 2nd ed. (Englewood Cliffs, N.J.: Prentice-Hall, 1989), p. 584. It proved too difficult to reconstruct the ensemble for this book. Again, I have preferred to retain the actual captions rather than create an ensemble of my own.

2. Cleanth Brooks, "*The Waste Land*: Critique of the Myth," in Cleanth Brooks, *Modern Poetry and the Tradition* (Chapel Hill: University of North Carolina Press, 1939), pp. 139–40.

3. Florence Jones, "T. S. Eliot among the Prophets," *American Literature* 38 (November 1966): 286–87, also reprinted in Lois A. Cuddy and David H. Hirsch, eds., *Critical Essays on T. S. Eliot's "The Waste Land"* (Boston: G. K. Hall, 1991). Page numbers refer to the original publication.

4. In the article by Florence Jones, the complete text of the second stanza is quoted. See Jones, "T. S. Eliot among the Prophets," p. 290.

5. Ibid., pp. 290–92.

6. Jewel Spears Brooker and Joseph Bentley, *Reading "The Waste Land": Modernism and the Limits of Interpretation* (Amherst: University of Massachusetts Press, 1990), pp. 67–68.

11. An Alchemy of Practice

1. The origins of this particular formulation of the properties of an algorithm have been impossible for me to trace; my successive reworking and arranging of the properties may have made the list close to some source no longer available to me. I claim no originality for the list, refer the reader to texts on computer science, and offer apologies and a promise of citation in subsequent editions should I be informed of its origins.

2. Because the sense of the stanza trades on the shifting between the singular (the listener) and the generality (our civilization, all people), a singular pronoun has been used throughout the discussion in this section. The text's "Son of man" invites the consistent use of the masculine pronoun, although the phrase itself and the surrounding lines are intended to refer to the condition of all people.

3. Jewel Spears Brooker and Joseph Bentley, *Reading "The Waste Land": Modernism and the Limits of Interpretation* (Amherst: University of Massachusetts Press, 1990), p. 65.

4. Florence Jones, "T. S. Eliot among the Prophets," *American Literature* 38 (November 1966): 290.

5. Ibid., p. 291.

6. Brooker and Bentley, *Reading "The Waste Land,"* p. 68.

7. Grover Smith, *T. S. Eliot's Poetry and Plays: A Study in Sources and Meaning* (Chicago: University of Chicago Press, 1956), pp. 73–74. In Smith's quotation from *The Waste Land*, the bracketed words and punctuation were omitted.

8. This discussion borrows heavily from Harold Garfinkel's articulation of classical sociology and ethnomethodology as providing two alternative, asymmetric technologies for the investigation of the problem of social order.

9. Dudley Fitts, "Fortunatus the R. A.," in Dudley Fitts, *Poems from the Greek Anthology in English Paraphrase* (New York: New Directions, 1956), p. 91.

10. Some have suggested that the notes were appended in order to make the poem long enough to be published as a separate book. See Hugh Kenner, *The Invisible Poet: T. S. Eliot* (London: Methuen and Co., 1959), pp. 129–30.

11. John B. Vickery, *The Literary Impact of "The Golden Bough"* (Princeton: Princeton University Press, 1973), pp. 248–49.

12. Geoffrey Chaucer, *The Prologue and Three Tales*, edited with notes and commentary by Francis King and Bruce Steele (Melbourne: F. W. Cheshire, 1969), pp. 1–2. The paraphrase is my own, but I have used King and Steele's notes as an aid.

13. Elizabeth Drew, *T. S. Eliot: The Design of His Poetry* (New York: Charles Scribner's Sons, 1949), p. 68.

14. Calvin Bedient, *He Do the Police in Different Voices: "The Waste Land" and Its Protagonist* (Chicago: University of Chicago Press, 1986), p. 26.

15. Ibid.

16. Other critics have claimed the presence of multiple voices, and have parsed and annotated the text accordingly as part of instructed readings, with the accompanying difficulties for laic reading in doing so. See, for example, Kenner, *The Invisible Poet*, pp. 135–37. Ultimately, however, Bedient wishes to see all the voices as being enacted by a single protagonist. See Bedient, *He Do the Police*.

12. The Technologies and Politics of Reading

1. See chap. 11, n. 8. To some extent, the material in this chapter reflects general themes in ethnomethodology and in ethnomethodological studies of work; the idea throughout this book, however, has been to speak concretely and in detail of the practices of reading and of critical reading, therein providing the grounds for claims about reading *simpliciter* and reading *cultura*. Ethnomethodology's strongest recom-

mendation may lie in such circumstances, that serious ethnomethodological work is not about something called "ethnomethodology" but about the worldly practices of the ordinary society, that the recommendations for such studies lie in real-worldly investigations and not in a supporting, academic literature. In addition to the debt to Garfinkel, there is a generalized debt to Harvey Sacks, to Melvin Pollner, and to ethnomethodological culture as a whole.

2. The expression "classical topics of order" is used by Garfinkel to refer to a similar situation in sociology, the reference being to topics such as "structure," "function," "logic," "meaning," "method," and "order" itself.

3. I borrow the expression "autobiographical image" from Melvin Pollner, who, in his lectures at UCLA in the early 1970s, described and analyzed a particular relationship between an objective world order and an "inquiring subject" as "mundane inquiry's autobiographical account of itself."

4. Wilfred Owen, *The Collected Poems of Wilfred Owen*, edited with an Introduction and Notes by C. Day Lewis and with a Memoir by Edmund Blunden (London: Chatto and Windus, 1963), p. 142.

5. The writings of Michael Riffaterre seem compatible with the study of reading found in this book; in fact, the discovered "distortion" of reading that is essential to the poetic object may be the fundamental insight behind Riffaterre's theoretics of poetry. I admire his readings of texts (as they are available to me in English translation) and would need to examine his writings and to consider his theorizing more carefully before advancing an opinion on them. I point to his work only as an example of a tremendous sensitivity to reading's work, of beautiful critical readings, and of a tendency toward such a disengaged theory.

6. See Stanley E. Fish, "Literature in the Reader: Affective Stylistics," *New Literary History* 2, no. 1 (Autumn 1970): 123–62, reprinted in Jane P. Tompkins, ed., *Reader-Response Criticism: From Formalism to Post-Structuralism* (Baltimore: John Hopkins University Press, 1980), pp. 70–100.

INDEX OF EXAMPLES

ERIC LIVINGSTON is Lecturer in Sociology at the University of New England, Armidale, New South Wales, Australia. He is the author of *The Ethnomethodological Foundations of Mathematics* and *Making Sense of Ethnomethodology*.